Notes on English Literature

Chief Adviser: JOHN D. JUMP
Professor of English Literature in the University of Manchester
General Editor: W. H. MASON
Lately Senior English Master, Manchester Grammar School

THE CRUCIBLE
(ARTHUR MILLER)

C. J. PARTRIDGE
B.A., Ph.D.

Assistant Professor, Department of English,
University of Victoria, B.C., Canada

BASIL BLACKWELL
OXFORD

© *Basil Blackwell 1971*

0 631 94760 4

PRINTED IN GREAT BRITAIN BY
WESTERN PRINTING SERVICES LTD, BRISTOL
AND BOUND BY KEMP HALL BINDERY, OXFORD

CONTENTS

iii

GENERAL NOTE

This series of introductions to the great classics of English literature is designed primarily for the school, college, and university student, although it is hoped that they will be found helpful by a much larger audience. Three aims have been kept in mind:

(A) To give the reader the relevant information necessary for his fuller understanding of the work.

(B) To indicate the main areas of critical interest, to suggest suitable critical approaches, and to point out possible critical difficulties.

(C) To do this in as simple and lucid a manner as possible, avoiding technical jargon and giving a full explanation of any critical terms employed.

Each introduction contains questions on the text and suggestions for further reading. It should be emphasized that in no sense is any introduction to be considered as a substitute for the reader's own study, understanding, and appreciation of the work.

NOTE

Unless otherwise stated, all page references are to the Penguin edition (1968) of *The Crucible*.

I

ACCUSATIONS, PROSECUTIONS, HYSTERIAS

The year 1953, which saw the inauguration of President Eisenhower in the United States and the death of Joseph Stalin in the Soviet Union, opened ominously. The first production of *The Crucible* at the Martin Beck Theatre, New York, conveyed an atmosphere of ominousness which may be related not only to the play's historical setting but also to the contemporary twentieth-century scene. It was almost eight years since the ending of a war which had achieved global dimensions. More than any previous war, the conflict from 1939–45 had taught that no person was exempt: the civilian non-combatant, whether disabled ex-soldier in the factory or the woman employed in agriculture, had contributed to the struggle taking place in the front lines. Enemy strategy had sometimes been concerned with affecting the morale of the civilian population on the assumption that such action, if successful, would affect the combativeness of troops at the front. For the major countries engaging in this conflict the mass media of radio, newspaper and cinema had been used to goad civilians to greater efforts in the total military commitment.

Now, at the beginning of 1953, the alliances which had brought victory over fascism in Germany, Italy and Japan were in shreds. Two super-powers, the United States and the Soviet Union, which had conducted the military struggle with varying degrees of mutual help, had become antagonistic to each other. Each had consolidated its influence over

1

large parts of the world so that in this period of 'cold war', under the mask of various 'defence' treaties, two new empires of enormous geographical and industrial magnitude appeared—one controlled by the United States and the other by the Soviet Union. The atmosphere of the cold war years had been acutely sensed by George Orwell who, in his novel *Nineteen Eighty-Four*, had imagined this condition extending into future time: the world was dominated by super-powers; these were regularly at war over obscure patches of territory so that civilians, in time of 'peace', lived with an abiding awareness of hostile enemies.

In the post-1945 period of imperial consolidation two ideologies glared with simplistic arrogance at each other across iron curtain, bamboo curtain and the tables of many international conference halls. In the East, communism appeared offering a messianic humanism to the poor and oppressed; in the West, capitalism, now re-named 'free enterprise', was preoccupied with re-defining its aims and stressing its essentially 'natural' and democratic evolution. To be a loyal communist in a communist country received approbation from those who controlled social and political change; to be a loyal advocate and practitioner of free enterprise in a free enterprise economy received approbation from those who guarded such an ideology. The simplistic attitudes of the time were endorsed and promulgated by the mass media so that, as in the preceding period of physical war, total commitment to the prevailing ideology was enjoined upon all citizens. In such an atmosphere to be suspected of sympathy for capitalism in a communist economy, or for communism in a free enterprise economy, could bring upon the suspect sudden trial, and rapid death or a lingering social disgrace. In such an atmosphere questions of loyalty can assume paramount importance. The real or alleged intrigues of spies can be dramatized by the media for public consumption and thus, by processes of persuasion and intimidation, the majority of the people are encouraged to remain in conformity to the existing social system. In the popular mind of North America and Western Europe there was a sudden vogue in fiction and films for the spy thriller, replacing to a large extent the previous popularity in the thirties and forties of murder mystery and 'private eye' narratives. The hidden criminal whose secrets must be revealed was no longer an individualistic killer with a cunning mind, but the employee of some international agency, frequently Russian in origin, concerned with weakening the defences of the hero's own country. It is a style which has influenced popular fiction and films to the present time.

In actual fact spies seemed to emerge from romantic obscurity into harsh reality—a reality which meant execution for some. In the opening weeks of 1953 recollections of past spy trials and warnings about the possibility of future ones were reiterated in the newspapers of many nations. The United States had earlier executed persons convicted of spying for the Soviet Union; in Czechoslovakia prominent communist leaders had recently been executed on charges of sabotaging their country's economy and intriguing for the return of capitalism; in the Soviet Union a new plot was being discovered in which doctors were conspiring against the life of Comrade Stalin.

This sense of continual conspiracy and intrigue makes the years of the late forties and early fifties a dark grotesque period when hypocrisy seemed institutionalized and individuals crushed beneath a new type of fear. It was a fear based on ideology and each citizen had to examine his conscience to find where he stood: the examination was conducted not before God, but before the prevailing ideology of the empire within which he lived.

When Arthur Miller reflected on this atmosphere, which he dramatized within a historical setting in *The Crucible*, he wrote in ironic and disparaging terms of imposed ideological conformity:

> Only England has held back before the temptations of contemporary diabolism. In the countries of the Communist ideology, all resistance of any import is linked to the totally malign capitalist succubi, and in America any man who is not reactionary in his views is open to the charge of alliance with the Red Hell. Political opposition, thereby, is given an inhumane overlay which then justifies the abrogation of all normally applied customs of civilized intercourse. A political policy is equated with moral right, and opposition to it with diabolical malevolence. Once such an equation is effectively made, society becomes a congerie of plots and counterplots, and the main role of government changes from that of the arbiter to that of the scourge of God.   (*The Crucible*, p. 38)

It is significant that, as we have done, Miller surveys various countries which share the dubious privilege of destroying the 'customs of civilized intercourse.' This phenomenon may appear in any place, at any time. In his own country the conflict between a political 'moral right' and a 'diabolical malevolence' had recently provoked the appearance of McCarthyism.

Appealing to American nationalist sentiment, Senator

Joseph McCarthy conducted hearings in which selected fellow-citizens were accused of possession, or of having possessed in the past, communist sympathies. Spies, trained agents of Russian intelligence networks, were thought to function in the most exalted branches of government and the mass media. They were infiltrating American life, affecting government decision-making, and influencing honest citizens through their presence in the communications media. As a consequence, it was asserted, American defence had been undermined. Many professional men and women, including motion picture celebrities, were arraigned in this period, urged to confess their true affiliations and reveal the names of acquaintances whom they regarded as communist sympathisers. In a short time reputations were damaged, careers ruined. A spate of books began to appear which were public—and probably well-paid—confessions by individuals who had been members of the communist party; they were now only too anxious to express disillusionment and show methods for dealing with such a subversive organization. These were the collaborators of the McCarthyite investigators, or 'witch-hunters'. Those who refused collaboration endured ordeal by slander, deprivation of jobs and, in some cases, preferred temporary exile abroad to further existence in the United States.

Within American historical experience the appearance of McCarthyism was particularly distressing. A country dedicated to liberty seemed suddenly to have negated its own ideals. Dissent from the prevailing ideology was perilous. And yet, could liberty continue to exist without the freedom to express dissent? Many Americans were bewildered and considerable bewilderment afflicted also foreign observers of the American scene, especially those in Western Europe who, having been encouraged to see the United States as protector of freedom and the Soviet Union as trampling upon individual rights, were forced to make new assessments of contemporary political values. One letter-writer to *The New Statesman and Nation* (10 January, 1953), comparing the execution of suspected traitors and spies in Czechoslovakia and the United States expressed the puzzlement of many:

> I wonder about the Prague trials, but I get indignant about the American witch-hunts. . . I think as deeply as newspapers can prepare me for thought. . . The Prague trials take some swallowing—but I can swallow them and point retaliatingly to the Rosenberg and Lattimore trials in the United States. What does this mean?

This distant, anonymous spectator was seeking intellectually to satisfy his own conscience somewhat like a protagonist in a play by Arthur Miller.

When Miller himself looked back on the corrupt and self-corrupting atmosphere of the early fifties he wrote in *After the Fall* (produced 1964) of two Americans who had had previous communist sympathies. In the period of political investigation one was willing to reveal the names of past associates to the committee; his friend Lou would be incriminated if he did this and, on hearing of the possibility, Lou exclaims: 'If everyone broke faith there would be no civilization! That is why the Committee is the face of the Philistine!'

Characteristically, and in a manner which is central for understanding *The Crucible*, Miller *goes behind* the reality of the immediate situation; instead of writing a documentary-style account of the 'witch-hunt' by the committee, he seeks to dramatize 'principles' of human behaviour inherent in a civilized society. The 'principle' of keeping faith and not handing one's conscience, as on a plate, to interrogators preserves the 'customs of civilized intercourse.' To break faith—that is, collaborate with, or confess to, the interrogators—may lead to the destruction of civilization. In this dramatized dilemma of conscience there is an element of autobiography, for Miller was himself one of the victims of political investigation.

Born into a Jewish-American family in New York in 1915, Arthur Miller was to see as a young man the catastrophic effects of the depression upon his family during the nineteen-thirties. The economic crisis and consequent austerity forced upon parents, relatives and people generally aroused in him a sense of social justice. The machine of government was not perfect and, when dislocation occurred, many who were innocent could suffer. There was thus built into Miller's artistic consciousness an awareness of social problems—of justice and injustice operating beyond the confines of a family.

In this respect he is different from many contemporary younger dramatists who, as products of less dislocated and more affluent societies, focus upon relationships and contradictions in relationships between people. This may be clarified by a brief quotation from the young British playwright Tom Stoppard. When addressing an audience at the National Union of Students' Drama Festival at Bradford in 1967 he stated:

As for real social stuff which makes headlines, I haven't

got the slightest desire to write about it on its own terms. . . My intention still is to write a play to commemorate, probably rather sceptically, the fiftieth anniversary of the Russian revolution. I started it about the beginning of 1966; but confronted with the enormous importance and reality of that revolution, I absolutely boggle, I don't know what to do about it. I think I want to write about that lovely group of octogenarians who I believe inhabit a house in Bayswater, who had to flee in 1917 and who are hanging about waiting for the whole thing to blow over so that they can go back.

('Something to Declare', *The Sunday Times*, 28 February, 1968.)

There is a division, as it were, between his own artistic preoccupations and the social world outside: the latter, with its upheavals and political struggles, may or may not be an artistic concern of Tom Stoppard.

Such an attitude is contrary to that found in the first period of Arthur Miller's writing. The agonies of social disharmony could not be evaded by one who had experienced the effects of economic dislocation. They need not be dramatized in the manner of a propagandist polemic, but some means of constructing a 'bridge' between the private drama of the family and the public drama of social issues had to be made. In his first modestly successful play *All My Sons* (produced 1947) this concern is demonstrated by showing the contradiction that may exist between an entrepreneur seeing responsibility in terms of his family's advantage and possessing an inadequate sense of responsibility towards the society at large. Joe Keller may profit and thrive from selling defective engine parts from his factory to the military; but twenty-one young pilots are killed. A contemporary younger dramatist might focus upon the 'absurdity' of such a situation and stress Keller's relationship with family and friends. Miller stresses the protagonists's lack of 'relatedness' to society beyond his family and friends. This may be expressed in Miller's own terms:

> The fortress which *All My Sons* lays siege to is the fortress of unrelatedness. It is an assertion not so much of a morality in terms of right and wrong, but of a moral world's being such because men cannot walk away from certain of their deeds.
>
> (Introduction, *Collected Plays* (1957), p. 19.)

The problems of 'relatedness' and responsibility are given further treatment in Miller's next play, *Death of a Salesman* (produced 1949). If an unsuccessful salesman is impelled by false dreams and an intensity of commitment to those dreams, what is the 'relatedness' between himself and his society? To what extent is the society itself at fault for endorsing the falsity and how may an individual—this sensitive 'bridge' between family and social nexus—survive as a living person? His essential integrity is at stake and failure to understand and change his condition may result in death.

We have outlined some aspect of social-political attitudes existing in various parts of the world in the early fifties. After the successful presentation of *Death of a Salesman* Miller became a prominent and famous playwright. But events were soon to cast shadows over this temporary triumph. He commented: 'If the reception of *All My Sons* and *Death of a Salesman* had made the world a friendly place for me, events of the early fifties quickly turned that warmth into an illusion' (Introduction, *Collected Plays*, p. 39). His involvement with a narrow dogmatic orthodoxy which sought to accuse him of un-American and pro-communist activities was to last until August, 1958, when he finally won an appeal against conviction for contempt of court. The conviction had been brought against Miller because he refused to divulge the names of fellow-writers who were present at meetings of communist party sym-pathisers held fifteen or more years previously. A few extracts from the official transcript of the interrogation held in 1956 conveys the tone of the questioning and Miller's attitude towards the proceedings. It may help us to appre-ciate the cross-examination of John Proctor in *The Crucible*.

MR. A: What occasioned your presence? Who invited you there?

MR. MILLER: I couldn't tell you. I don't know.

MR. A: Can you tell us who was there when you walked into the room?

MR. MILLER: . . . I am not protecting the Communists or the Communist Party. I am trying to and I will protect my sense of myself. I could not use the name of another person and bring trouble on him. . . I will tell you any-thing about myself, as I have.

MR. A: These were Communist Party meetings, were they not?

MR. MILLER: I will be perfectly frank with you in anything relating to my activities. I take the responsibility for everything I have ever done, but I cannot take respon-sibility for another human being.

MR. A: This record shows, does it not, Mr. Miller, that these were Communist Party meetings?

It is unlikely that at this late stage in the hearings Miller could have revealed any names not already known to the committee. His refusal to cooperate was motivated by the principle of not collaborating with, or confessing to, inquisitors dogmatically imposing an ideological conformity.

For Miller the outcome brought some satisfaction: he had not been forced into exile or to work under assumed names—as were the fates of some Hollywood writers and film directors caught up in the series of solemn denunciations. He had carried himself with dignity and lived to see the end of the McCarthyite phenomenon. But preservation of his own integrity—and, by implication, of a value in civilized intercourse—was not seen by himself as an absolute victory. In 1960 he remarked during an interview for a London newspaper: 'When you don't defeat somebody on the basis of principle, he is only personally defeated, that's all. His ghost goes marching on so long as the lesson has not been learned in terms of the principles that he is violating. And the defeat of McCarthy was never on that basis for the majority.' (*The Sunday Times*, 20 March, 1960.)

It was towards an examination of principle within such a phenomenon of accusations, prosecutions and hysteria that he had devoted his efforts in writing *The Crucible* in 1952. His awareness, as we have seen, was of a problem existing beyond the confines of his own country. When political policy is dogmatically buttressed by a sense of 'moral right'—a military-bueraucratic attitude which often characterizes expanding or consolidating empires—opposition to that policy may come to be seen as 'diabolical': the mass of people might then evince symptoms of hysteria, aligning themselves with the 'moral right', handing over their individual consciences to the care of political guardians, and accepting the condition of ideological conformity. What, then, is the 'relatedness' between a man of principle who refuses to do this and the society in which he lives? To whom is such a person responsible—the society with its conformist dogmatism, his family and friends, or his own conscience?

This experience, terrifying in its implications, was not new to history. In a Salem courthouse Miller had discovered a book written by a nineteenth-century clergyman analysing the Salem witchcraft trials of 1692; he found from his own study of the court records, some of which had been reproduced by the nineteenth-century historian, other instances of accusations, prosecutions and hysteria. His dramatic interest was aroused.

Extension projects:

(a) In our century many novels have been written about the power of governments to limit individual freedom. Some of these project events into a future time. The best-known is George Orwell's *Nineteen Eighty-Four*; Orwell was influenced to some extent by a Russian writer, Evgeni Zamiatin, whose novel *We* had been written in 1920–21. (This is most readily available in B. G. Guerney's *Anthology of Russian Literature in the Soviet Period*, Random House, 1960.) In these fictional representations of future life an all-powerful, all-controlling committee of guardians possesses the 'moral right' to suppress dissent and see opponents of the government as diabolically malevolent. It might be interesting to compare these pessimistic evocations of the future with Arthur Miller's evocation of a witch-hunt atmosphere in *The Crucible*. What do these works have in common and what questions of principle are being brought forward to our attention?

(b) *The Crucible* opened at the Royal Court Theatre, London, on 9 April, 1956. If your public library has retained back issues of periodicals and newspapers try to determine what were reviewers' comments on the play. What exactly were the reactions published in *The New Statesman and Nation*, *The Spectator*, *The Times*, *The Sunday Times*, *The Observer*?

(c) To learn something of Arthur Miller's general attitude to life and society it may be interesting to read the interview published in *The Sunday Times*, 20 March, 1960.

Question:

Write your first impressions of *The Crucible*. After a first reading what seem to you the essential issues of the drama?

II

AN ATMOSPHERE OF DREAD

It sometimes happens that the idea for a work of art occurs to the intending writer, painter, musician at a comparatively early age while the young person is still at school or university. The idea may lie dormant for decades while other projects occupy the difficult years of artistic apprenticeship. Then, at a crucial moment in the artist's life, the earlier idea reappears in his mind with new forcefulness and the complex process of shaping the material into significant form begins. Miller had been interested in the strange events which had taken place more than two centuries previously in Salem, Massachusetts, when he was still an adolescent in high school; but it was that crisis in his experience provoked by the atmosphere of dread in the early nineteen-fifties which prompted his interest to return to the Puritan colonial world.

It is important to understand the 'image' which Miller has of the Salem community. In his commentary at the beginning of Act One he describes it as a theocracy—'a combine of state and religious power whose function was to keep the community together, and to prevent any kind of disunity that might open it to destruction by material or ideological enemies' (p. 16). In other words, power was in the hands of a small group concerned with maintaining unity amidst the rigours of new-world life. Individual dissent was not permitted and, when the common unity was *thought* to be threatened, the guardians of society and many citizens over-reacted in their confusion, thus adding panic to panic, hysteria to hysteria. In the resultant disorder, opportunity was provided for smouldering jealousies between acquaintances to kindle, neighbours to covet neighbours' goods, and false accusations of witchcraft to be made against others in the hope of personal, economic gains. As Miller ironically says: 'Old scores could be settled on a plane of heavenly combat between Lucifer and the Lord; suspicions and the envy of the miserable toward the happy could and did burst out in the general revenge' (p. 17). All that had seemed 'natural' and guided by Providence in the community was now perversely infected by the dark powers of disorder.

In historical fact a disorder of considerable proportions had afflicted the village of Salem in 1692. Public feelings boiled to such an intensity in this crucible of emotion that few citizens escaped: not only the Salem community but also other outlying villages underwent a period of severe trial. Parents were incarcerated in jails, children left destitute and homes despoiled. Nineteen people were executed on charges of witchcraft and one, Giles Corey, was crushed to death. And yet the crisis in this, as in so many human situations, had grown from small beginnings.

During 1691 and 1692 a number of young girls, meeting at the Reverend Parris's house, had formed a group to practise palmistry and fortune-telling. Mr. Parris, who formerly had lived in the West Indies, had two slaves, one of whom was Tituba. She came to exercise some influence over the girls. Among these were Abigail Williams (in 1692 aged about twelve) and Mary Warren, a servant in John

Proctor's household. It is possible that they and the other girls acted out of boredom with the rigid standards of behaviour in the puritan community; they sought in such pastimes as palmistry and fortune-telling an excitement not permitted by the standards of the society. Perhaps they were expressing the rebellious instincts of adolescence by such additional acts as dancing at night in the surrounding forest—an area regarded by the Puritan adults as the domain of the devil.

When rumours of these activities began to spread, the girls may have attempted to continue their rebellious behaviour by making accusations against prominent adults; alternatively, perhaps the first accusations were prompted by self-defence and fear of punishment. Whatever their inner motives—and they are unlikely ever to be accurately ascertained—the young people came to be looked upon by the inhabitants of Salem village as 'the afflicted girls'. The local physician Dr. Griggs said they were bewitched, thus ascribing 'diabolical' causes to the convulsive spasms and sharp cries which now characterized their appearances in public. The nineteenth-century historian, C. W. Upham, whose work *Salem Witchcraft* (1867) Miller read during his study of the phenomenon, describes their behaviour in this way:

They would creep into holes, and under benches and chairs, put themselves into odd and unnatural postures, make wild and antic gestures, and utter incoherent and unintelligible sounds. They would be seized with spasms, drop insensible to the floor, or writhe in agony, suffering dreadful tortures, and uttering loud and piercing outcries.

The general ascription of witchcraft to 'the afflicted girls' spread rapidly through the community and surrounding countryside.

The Puritan theocracy and many ordinary citizens held the theory that evil spirits could adversely affect human society; the devil and his minions operated on humanity by using certain individuals. These 'witches', it was believed, could infect the good and the innocent—such as the young girls—spreading by these 'afflicted' ones a contagion which, like a plague, might destroy a previously wholesome, God-guided community. No person was exempt from charges of witchcraft: church-members of all social strata, persons eminent in charitable acts, such as Sarah Good, people of all ages were capable of joining with the devil and becoming active agents in a monstrous conspiracy against orthodoxy and order. Accusations and counter-accusations added to the atmosphere of dread; with the growth of fear there developed mass-hysteria and the attendant wish to search for, and destroy, the malignant spirits.

It may be seen that there was a strong tendency in the intellectual outlook of both leaders and people to behave in the manner of the physician Dr. Griggs. Unable, or unwilling, to give a medical cause of the spasms and contortions which the young girls showed, they gave a metaphysical and theological explanation stressing diabolical malevolence. So deeply influenced by a narrow dogmatism, they were incapable of perceiving simple causes for events; their ideological view confused them, so that a conspiracy was felt on all sides, and fanaticism replaced reason. In Arthur Miller's perspective, the social tragedy which he dramatized in *The Crucible* was 'the everlasting conflict between people so fanatically wedded to this orthodoxy

that they could not cope with the evidence of their senses.'
(*The Saturday Review*, 31 January, 1953.)

Although *The Crucible* should never be seen as a
mechanical parable about McCarthyite America, the atmosphere of dread in the Salem of 1692 may be paralleled
with the world of the late nineteen-forties and early
nineteen-fifties. We have outlined some of the factors
contributing to this ominousness in both periods and shall
now examine in detail the manner in which Miller dramatizes this mood of fear and repression.

All the names used in *The Crucible* are authentic, as are
the fates of the persons. However, as little is really known
of the villagers' lives or temperaments, the characters behind the names have been 'rounded out' by Miller's
dramatic imagination.

The spring of 1692 did not produce an awareness of new
life or new vigour for the inhabitants of Salem. In the opening scene the morning sunlight streams through a narrow
window in the Reverend Parris's house. It casts only a
small light into a room of sparse austerity. Although
objects are carefully arranged about the room, suggesting
a clerical order and self-discipline, a contrast between light
and dark is immediately conveyed to a spectator. The
middle-aged minister prays against the dark sickness which
afflicts his daughter. He is distraught at a sense of disorder
which he fears is entering his home. His peremptory dismissal of the black slave Tituba and his semi-coherent
prayers dramatize, by broken phrases and abrupt rhythms,
both the pain in his mind and the ominous invading disorder.

The entry of Susanna Walcott—nervously, hurriedly—

adds to these implications of disruption. She has come direct from Doctor Griggs; the physician is reported as advising—in the manner the court records report the historical Doctor Griggs—that the father 'might look to unnatural things for the cause' (p. 18) of his daughter's sickness. Parris is further pained at the suggestion, repeating the word 'unnatural' several times, thus setting up, as it were, ominous reverberations in the mind of a spectator.

Parris has reason to be apprehensive. He knows his daughter Betty, his adopted niece Abigail Williams and his slave Tituba, all members of his 'orderly' household, have danced at night in the forest—in the popular imagination that 'disorderly' domain of the devil. Now, as Abigail tells him, 'the rumour of witchcraft is all about' (p. 18) and Parris fears that enemies in the parish may conspire to remove him from his ministry.

Unfortunately, his fears are compounded with the appearance of Mrs. Putnam. She bursts into the room, breaking apart the slender restoration of order which Parris has been trying to achieve through his conversations with Susanna Walcott and Abigail Williams. Mrs. Putnam enters as a positive force, convinced of diabolical malevolence in the community. Her first words are aimed directly at the minister:

MRS. PUTNAM (*full of breath, shiny-eyed*): It is a marvel. It is surely a stroke of hell upon you.
PARRIS: No, Goody Putnam, it is—
MRS. PUTNAM (*glancing at Betty*): How high did she fly, how high?
PARRIS: No, no, she never flew— (p. 21)

The imagery she uses in her following comments conveys both her own conviction of the devil's presence and the positive incursion of disorder into the 'clean spareness' of the Puritan community. The Reverend Parris's daughter, she asserts, has been seen flying over a barn and alighting like a bird. Her own daughter, Ruth, is also sick; but 'with vicious certainty' she states that this is no natural sickness:

> I'd not call it sick: the Devil's touch is heavier than sick. It's death, y'know, it's death drivin' into them, forked and hoofed.   (p. 21)

Parris's self-assurance dwindles before the certainty of Mrs. Putnam and her husband. Already he begins to assume a defensive posture, almost pleading with Thomas Putnam not to assert the presence of unnatural elements:

> Thomas, Thomas, I pray you, leap not to witchcraft. I know that you—you least of all, Thomas, would ever wish so disastrous a charge laid upon me. We cannot leap to witchcraft. They will howl me out of Salem for such corruption in my house.   (p. 22)

The minister's tone of intense pleading is the more understandable when it is realized that Thomas Putnam has been one of his main supporters in the village. When disagreements broke out, Thomas Putnam sided with him and Parris knows his indebtedness to, and reliance on, this influential man of the parish.

The Putnams are a strange couple. Thomas is wealthy but seems to have an obsession with influencing other people and hence making his will prevail in the community. He continually intrigues over land, seeking to increase his already large holdings but, ironically, of the couple's eight children seven have died. Now the surviving child, Ruth, is sick. There is consequently the possibility of no heir to the family fortune. Mrs. Putnam is desperate. She is convinced that unnatural forces have caused the deaths of her children. In her desperation she has sent Ruth to Tituba who, it is thought, can speak with the dead to learn who has murdered all her offspring (p. 23). It was a curious recourse for this forty-five-year-old Christian woman to seek help from the pagan (obeah) beliefs of a West Indian slave.

The first impression of Ann Putnam on a spectator can only be unsympathetic. The imagery suggestive of witch-craft and devilry which marks her initial appearance conveys her outer hardness of assertion and fanatical conviction. But there is a terrible pathos behind this outer hardness— a pathos which is revealed by her words to the minister when she relates the misfortunes attending her children:

> I have laid seven babies unbaptized in the earth. Believe me, sir, you never saw more hearty babies born. And yet, each would wither in my arms the very night of their birth. I have spoke nothin', but my heart has clamoured intimations. And now, this year, my Ruth, my only— I see her turning strange. A secret child she has become this year, and shrivels like a sucking mouth were pullin' on her life too. And so I thought to send her to your Tituba— (p. 23)

The simple language and cadenced phrases, like the gasp of a woman whose life has become one long sob, beauti-fully express the frustrated tenderness of a mother deprived of giving love to her children.

With the Putnams' accusations that witches are at work murdering members of the community, Reverend Parris feels a 'frantic terror' (p. 24): there is an imputation that Tituba and possibly Abigail are involved. Putnam encourages him to proclaim publicly the discovery of witchcraft. Parris is swayed but seeks a temporary compromise; he will lead the villagers in a psalm, but will not yet announce the presence of witches.

As his character is revealed through the events of Act One, he is shown as a man with a basic insecurity. This tends to make him compromising and subservient before men of influence such as Putnam. When criticized by social inferiors among his parishioners, however, his essential insecurity makes him emphasize his status and clerical rights; material goods are the outward expression of his status and Parris has been prepared to squabble over his salary and provision of firewood (p. 34), and to demand the deed of the house in which he lives (p. 34). His insecurity is heightened by a sense of persecution—a faction conspiring against him—and, as a man possessing unsure authority, he exaggerates the role of authority in the community. Preaching 'hellfire and bloody damnation' (p. 34), he asserts: 'There is either obedience or the church will burn like Hell is burning!' (p. 35)

The insecurity of such a nature may become a dangerous thing when it is felt that conspiracies are growing on all sides to undermine one's status and authority. Parris exclaims:

> You will look far for a man of my kind at sixty pound a year! I am not used to this poverty; I left a thrifty business in the Barbados to serve the Lord. I do not fathom

it, why am I persecuted here? I cannot offer one proposition but there be a howling riot of argument. I have often wondered if the Devil be in it somewhere; I cannot understand you people otherwise. (p. 34)

Such petulance assumes ominous overtones when, like Dr. Griggs, Reverend Parris is readily willing to ascribe 'unnatural' and diabolical causes to human activities.

In contrast to Parris's profound insecurity, Reverend John Hale enters the village of Salem and the Parris household with all the assurance that learning, and a reputation for learning, can provide. He is anxious to be of service. Insecurity may be the foundation of the Reverend Parris's appeals to authority: a whole edifice of knowledge is to be placed by the Reverend Hale at the service of the villagers.

But there is a defect in the type of learning and the mentality which Hale embodies. Despite vast quantities of thought and reading, his mind has failed to question the fundamental assumptions on which it rests. Reverend Hale has never questioned, for instance, the reality of the devil; upon the assumption that the devil exists and is always seeking to extend his malignant power, he has built his intellectual edifice. His knowledge supports an existing theological or ideological structure; it does not question that structure. Miller reminds us that in contemporary societies a communist intellectual may similarly never question the malignancy of capitalism, or an intellectual in Western Europe or North America may too rarely question the reputed evils of communism. As a consequence learning, no matter how vast and impressive, having failed to be

sceptical of basic assumptions, can easily appear hollow
and pretentious. Such is the effect of Reverend Hale's
learning—an effect made on his first appearance.

Miller describes him as being like 'a young doctor on his
first call. His painfully acquired armoury of symptoms,
catchwords, and diagnostic procedures are now to be put
to use at last' (p. 40). He enters burdened with his meta-
physician's tools—half a dozen heavy books which he
states in all seriousness are 'weighted with authority.'
Because he is so serious about his function, subtle touches
of comedy characterize Miller's initial presentation of
Reverend Hale. But it is a humour which few audiences
appreciate, so rapidly has the atmosphere of dread been
spreading in the opening encounters of the drama. His
mannered geniality and controlled friendliness, suggestive
of the professional physician, lead him to express his conviction of the need for 'hard study if it comes to tracking
down the Old Boy' (p. 40). This doctor is unlikely to be an
impartial diagnostician. Unexamined assumptions behind
his learning are leading him to ludicrous attitudes and
prejudiced deductions. These may be clearly seen by contrasting Hale's responses with the responses of Rebecca
Nurse to the same situation.

Before his arrival the old, uneducated woman Rebecca
had looked at the sick child. When Rebecca stood over her,
the child had stopped whimpering (p. 31). The old woman
commented: 'A child's spirit is like a child, you can never
catch it by running after it; you must stand still, and, for
love, it will soon itself come back' (p. 32). Her common
sense then deflates the Putnams' exaggerated anxieties and
contrasts with the growing irrational fear in the household.

MRS. PUTNAM: My Ruth is bewildered, Rebecca; she cannot eat.

REBECCA: Perhaps she is not hungered yet. (p. 32)

Very different is Hale's response when informed of Ruth Putnam's malady. A seriousness, so large that its implications to an audience are comic, characterizes his educated wonderment:

PUTNAM: We look to you to come to our house and save our child.

HALE: Your child ails too?

MRS. PUTNAM: Her soul, her soul seems flown away. She sleeps and yet she walks . . .

PUTNAM: She cannot eat.

HALE: Cannot eat! (*Thinks on it.*) (p. 41)

The common sense to say 'Perhaps she is not hungered yet' is buried beneath an edifice of learning which already tends towards searching out, and destroying, 'loose spirits.' His appearance of thoughtful impartiality has the effect of reinforcing a theological dogmatism; convinced that his books contain absolute truths, he asserts, 'with a tasty love of intellectual pursuit':

Here is all the invisible world, caught, defined, and calculated. In these books the Devil stands stripped of all his brute disguises. Here are all your familiar spirits— your incubi and succubi; your witches that go by land, by air, and by sea; your wizards of the night and of the day. Have no fear now—we shall find him out if he has come among us, and I mean to crush him utterly if he has shown his face! (*He starts for the bed.*) (p. 42)

The ponderous phrases, the complex sentence structure, the mediaeval-like categorizing of spirits by their mode of travel and the times of their manifestations—all add to the ludicrousness of the learned gentleman. But it is a ludicrousness which can be dangerous for his terrible intensity is serving, ironically, to increase fears—as is shown by the interrogation he now conducts.

His mental attitude determines his method of questioning people in order to learn the causes of the children's illnesses. The questions are always based on the assumption that the devil exists and has been exerting his 'precise' influence in the community, rather as the interrogation of Arthur Miller always assumed that any association with the communist party was malignant and destructive to the American people. Whatever answers are given the interrogator, they merely consolidate his fundamental prejudice, so that a seemingly innocent occurrence becomes evidence of diabolical activity.

This mental attitude and this method of questioning, which in the structure of the play anticipate the attitudes and methods pervading the courtroom in Act Three, add to the developing tension and hysteria. Hale is the demanding interrogator: the people in the Reverend Parris's household are on the defensive. Abigail is under immediate pressure and forced to assert that she has never sold herself to the devil: 'I'm a good girl! I'm a proper girl!' (p. 45)

The appearance of Tituba makes Abigail implicate the black woman; the drinking of chicken's blood is interpreted by Hale as a means by which the West Indian woman has used the children for the devil's purposes. She has 'sent out' the devil's spirit and it has infected the young people. Abigail adds to the mounting evidence: 'She sends her spirit on me in church; she makes me laugh at prayer. . . She comes to me every night to go and drink blood. . . She comes to me while I sleep; she's always making me dream corruptions!' (p. 46) The rhythmic similarity of the sentences and repetitions of accusations are creating a *crescendo* effect as the scene moves to its climactic close.

Predictably, Hale accepts all these assertions; he has found one woman who has made a compact with the devil. The pressure of questioning moves to her and, frightened by the possibility of death and by the self-righteous intensity of the white masters surrounding her, Tituba suggests that 'somebody else be witchin' these children.' (p. 47)

At this, a name is required and the atmosphere of interrogation changes to one of enforced confession. The black woman, tormented by her own terror, names Sarah Good and Goody Osburn; at this moment Abigail rises, adds another name and Betty, affected by the voices of the others, breaks her silence and utters further names. The act concludes as though it were the hysterical climax to a religious service—but a service very different from, and contrasting with, Reverend Parris's earlier recitation of a psalm. Names are called as though in a litany; but the effect of this calling is that reputations are destroyed and people are being put under threat of torture and execution. Interrogation has led to forced confessions, confessions to an atmosphere of perverted religious participation. The atmosphere of dread has become an active, fear-filled hysteria. Much of the hysteria is still confined to the small upper bedroom of Parris's house, but it is to spread to other homes and bring terror to many innocent parishioners.

Extension projects:

(a) Miller was not the first American writer to dramatize the events in Salem. Many novels have been written on the subject—none of them with abiding literary value. In 1868 the most famous and respected of American poets, Henry Wadsworth Longfellow, wrote a verse-tragedy on

> Delusions of the days that once have been,
> Witchcraft and wonders of the world unseen,
> Phantoms of air, and necromantic arts
> That crushed the weak and awed the stoutest hearts.

He chose Giles Corey as his protagonist and in stiff blank verse, and even stiffer dramatic action, showed events leading to Giles 'lying dead, with a great stone on his breast, the Sheriff at his head.'

Longfellow's dramas have fallen into obscurity, and deservedly so, as have the plays of his famous English contemporary, Alfred Tennyson. However, it may be interesting to read Longfellow's 'Giles Corey of the Salem Farms' to deduce the manner in which he fails as a dramatist. His lack of success may then contrast with the urgent dramatic power of Arthur Miller's writing. See Henry Wadsworth Longfellow, *The New England Tragedies* (1868).

(b) The historical account of the Salem trials by Charles W. Upham has been reprinted. Students of history may be interested in reading a nineteenth-century historian's view of the events.

Charles W. Upham, *Salem Witchcraft,* Boston, 1867 (reprinted New York, 1959).

A modern and more 'popular' account may be found in Marion L. Starkey, *The Devil in Massachusetts*, Robert Hale (London) 1952.

Questions:

1. Discuss Miller's use of irony as shown in the dramatic structure of Act One.

2. Discuss the changes in the atmosphere of the opening act. At what points does the mood change and how important is *tempo* for conveying these changes?

3. Make your own character study of Reverend Parris. To what extent would you agree that he possesses a basic insecurity?

4. Can any defence be made of Ann and Thomas Putnam's behaviour during Act One in their encounters with (a) Reverend Parris, (b) John Proctor, (c) Reverend Hale?

5. To what extent may John Hale be seen as a comic character in Act One?

6. How effectively, during the opening act, is irony used in the presentation of character?

7. 'The opening exposition is cluttered and clouded.'

'In the first act Miller shows remarkable dramatic skill in suggesting both a powerful social order and the incipient disruption of that order.'

Develop and discuss these critical assertions.

8. How effective is the climax to Act One? (You may be interested in writing notes on the staging of this part of the act: what devices of lighting, group movement, and perhaps music would you use for enhancing effect?)

III

AN INTERPLAY OF WOMEN:
ABIGAIL WILLIAMS, ELIZABETH PROCTOR

As he studied more carefully the records of what had taken place in Salem in 1692, Arthur Miller pondered the fact that a former servant-girl, Abigail, had incriminated her previous mistress by charges of witchcraft but had avoided involving the master of the house, John Proctor. There was no other record in the Salem court cases of a similarly divided accusation: husbands and wives usually suffered the same accusations and prosecutions. Why should this exception have been made? Miller's dramatic imagination was held by the question. Was there a hidden secret guilt between the three which was to become a fearful psychological weakness in a time of social disharmony? Miller invented such a secret guilt—an error in past behaviour for which a high price had to be paid during the present crisis—by making John Proctor guilty of an adulterous association with Abigail Williams.

It is important, at this point, to consider a statement Miller made about his 'central impulse' for writing *The Crucible*:

> The central impulse for writing at all was not the social but the interior psychological question, which was the question of that guilt residing in Salem which the hysteria merely unleashed, but did not create. Consequently, the structure reflects that understanding. . .

(Introduction, *Collected Plays* (1957), p. 42)

30

Perhaps Miller, in making these comments, was hoping to correct early impressions of the play by audiences and critics; reviewers of its first performances, in the United States and abroad, during the nineteen-fifties saw it as a 'parable' or 'allegory'—the words were used indiscriminately and without definition—of life in McCarthyite America.

From our later perspective it should be possible to see that the complexity of *The Crucible* derives in part from its being both a series of private, personal tragedies *and* a public, social tragedy. We have outlined Miller's concern with the problem of 'relatedness' between an individual and his society, have surveyed aspects of the social tragedy, and seen also the frailty of such 'strong' prominent people as Reverend Parris, the Putnams, Reverend Hale. Behind the exterior of each is an insecurity: Parris fears for his reputation and is apprehensive of retaining his position; Mr. Putnam is desirous always to extend his influence over others but, with his wife, ironically shares the guilt of having only one surviving child to 'influence' and to inherit his wealth; Reverend Hale may not yet be conscious of his own intellectual deficiencies, but his naïve seriousness and ludicrous intensity imply to an audience the uncertain sands on which his intellectual edifice has been built. (This is to be made explicit in the progression of events.) We shall now consider the characters and functions of Abigail Williams and Elizabeth Proctor, the two women most dramatically important in the play.

At first it may seem that Abigail Williams is primarily responsible for the climate of hysteria in Salem. But, as with so many situations in real life, the more one considers the origin of a phenomenon the more difficult it becomes to assign guilt and responsibility. One may try always to endorse the aphorism 'To understand all is to forgive all.' Is there anything that can be forgiven in so obviously malicious a character as Abigail?

The fictional Abigail is very beautiful, aged seventeen, and shows 'an endless capacity for dissembling' (p. 18). This capacity is clearly revealed during the progression of Act One and may be clarified by analysing her encounters with Reverend Parris, Reverend Hale and John Proctor.

Although Parris urges her to admit all the facts about the girls' activities in the forest, Abigail only pretends to state all she knows. Parris pleads with her, stating with dignity the seriousness of the situation and stressing the need for truth:

PARRIS: Now tell me true, Abigail. And I pray you feel the weight of truth upon you, for now my ministry's at stake, my ministry and perhaps your cousin's life. Whatever abomination you have done, give me all of it now, for I dare not be taken unaware when I go before them down there.

ABIGAIL: There is nothin' more. I swear it, uncle.   (p. 20)

However, when questioned later by Reverend Hale, it becomes evident she knows that 'something more' than 'common dancing' has taken place at the nocturnal meetings in the forest (pp. 45–46). Her revelations, leading to the incrimination of Tituba, show a dissembling so extensive on Abigail's part that considerable lying is necessary to support the appearance she wishes to present. She has lied to her benefactor Parris, despite his emphasis on the need for truth, and soon this capacity is to be used for incriminating other innocent people.

Superficially, she is anxious to pretend about her 'name', or reputation for integrity. Rumours of a relationship with John Proctor have circulated since her dismissal from service in the Proctor household. Parris has requested her to tell him the truth about this possible blemish on her reputation:

PARRIS: Your name in the town—it is entirely white, is it not?

ABIGAIL (*with an edge of resentment*): Why, I am sure it is, sir. There be no blush about my name. (p. 20)

She attributes any aspersion cast on her character to Elizabeth Proctor. Abigail claims that John's wife has tried to treat her like a slave and she pretends that she has rebelled against such an attitude, asserting, in a temper:

My name is good in the village! I will not have it said my name is soiled! Goody Proctor is a gossiping liar!

(p. 21)

But in the brief, dramatically tense dialogue between Abigail and John when they are alone with the sick child, their past adulterous relationship is made explicit. In this encounter Abigail is shown not only to have lied to her guardian but also to possess a passionate, desiring nature. She has a shrewd percipience in seeing John's weakness and an active willingness to manipulate this man to satisfy her own passion. She reminds him of his own deeply emotional nature, recalling their sexual experience; she asserts that he is no 'wintry' man (p. 29), and attributes (accurately as will be seen later) qualities of coldness, weakness and lack of passion to Elizabeth. She has referred to her earlier as 'a lying, cold, snivelling woman' (p. 20) and she repeats this to John.

ABIGAIL (*with a bitter anger*): Oh, I marvel how such a strong man may let such a sickly wife be—
PROCTOR (*angered—at himself as well*): You'll speak nothin' of Elizabeth!
ABIGAIL: She is blackening my name in the village! She is telling lies about me! She is a cold, snivelling woman, and you bend to her!   (pp. 29–30)

Abigail displays a remarkable firmness of purpose. Her passion, now frustrated by John's return to sexual fidelity, is a driving force—a violent, pent-up power which has given her temporary influence over Proctor and a larger influence over the other girls. She is the leader among them. When urged by Mary Warren to tell the truth about their activities in the forest and provoked further by Betty's garblings, she reasserts her domination by an act of violence. She takes the sick child who has wandered from the bed to the window and 'smashes her across the face' (p. 26). It is this tendency to violence which most deeply characterizes Abigail. The imagery she uses to describe imaginatively her sexual experience with Proctor suggests the mating of wild, hot, untamed animals:

I know how you clutched my back behind your house and sweated like a stallion whenever I come near! Or did I dream that? . . . A wild thing may say wild things.

But not so wild, I think. . . I have a sense for heat, John, and yours has drawn me to my window. . . I cannot sleep for dreamin'; I cannot dream but I wake and walk about the house as though I'd find you comin' through some door. (*She clutches him desperately.*) (p. 29)

Fulfilled passion may have offered a healthful integration of her emotions but, since John's rebuttal of her advances, the psychological violence is to break out into new manifestations. The extension of dissembling and lying is to arouse her innate violence and require increasing use of this disintegrative force. Unfortunately, the disintegrative force enters the community; other people's reputations are to be blemished, while Abigail's reputation for 'goodness' ironically grows.

Can any defence be made of such a person? It is important to remember that as a child she witnessed the murder of her parents:

I saw Indians smash my dear parents' heads on the pillow next to mine, and I have seen some reddish work done at night. (p. 27)

The impression of violence and its ineradicable finality seem to have remained with her. As an adolescent, to prosecute her private vengeance against Elizabeth Proctor, she connives at judicial murder. And this may seem no unnatural thing to Abigail. The success of her first denunciations, the later trickery to implicate Elizabeth by means of the doll, and her supreme commanding power in the courtroom merely convince her that the form of verbal violence she has by chance discovered is an extremely effective weapon. So effective is it, and so great is her final power in suggesting the violent presence of diabolical disorders, that she can perturb even Deputy Governor Danforth.

During the trial in Act Three, when Mary Warren has denied seeing spirits and, by implication, is invalidating the testimony of the girls, Danforth urges her to re-consider her previous statements. However, his suggestion that she may, unintentionally, have harboured illusions is rejected by Abigail as a 'base question' (p. 96). Her following utterances are vehement expostulations which contain further images of violence:

ABIGAIL: I have been hurt, Mr. Danforth; I have seen my blood runnin' out! I have been near to murdered every day because I done my duty pointing out the Devil's people—and this is my reward? To be mistrusted, denied, questioned like a—
DANFORTH (*weakening*): Child, I do not mistrust you—
(p. 96)

The all-powerful Danforth, for a moment, is made defensive; at this, Abigail asserts herself yet more by adopting an accusatory attitude to the Deputy Governor:

ABIGAIL (*in an open threat*): Let *you* beware, Mr. Danforth. Think you to be so mighty that the power of Hell may not turn *your* wits? Beware of it! (p. 96)

Shortly afterwards, when Proctor openly accuses *her* of plotting Elizabeth's death and enacting the vengeance of a whore, Danforth asks her if she will deny these charges. Abigail replies: 'If I must answer that, I will leave and I will not come back again!' (p. 98) The judge falters before this new disclosure and seems ready to doubt Abigail's evidence; at this point she steps up to him and asks, 'What look do you give me?' Danforth is unable to speak.

She is at the height of her power and can easily terrorize over Mary Warren's 'peeping courage'. When she manipulates the girls in the court, she is able to make Danforth 'horrified' (p. 102) so that even he grows hysterical (p. 102). In these encounters with her, his responses have been characterized by self-defensiveness, reduction to silence, and finally a degree of hysteria.

Abigail is a figure of human malevolence who, in the ironic reversals of humanistic values dramatized through the play's movements, is thought by some villagers and by the theocratic moral self-righteousness of the authorities to be a victim of circumstances. In one sense she may be such a victim: a luckless introduction to violence by the deaths of her parents has strengthened her will; her 'endless capacity for dissembling' has developed her art of duplicity so that, at the height of mass hysteria, she is a creature of supreme arrogance. John Proctor's words about Abigail— 'She is a lump of vanity, sir' (p. 98)—suggest a fundamental truth about her nature. Were it not for her power of life and death over many people, she is a person to be pitied rather than condemned.

The atmosphere in the Proctor household is strained, and its tensions and uncertainties are implied by several dramatic devices at the beginning of Act Two. Before any words are uttered, John's actions, prior to Elizabeth's entry, are indicative of a deficiency in their relationship. He walks to the fireplace, tastes some stew and finds it unsatisfactory. Not wishing his wife to know this, he adds some salt and moves away from the fireplace before she comes into the room. He then compliments his wife on her cooking: 'It's well seasoned.' (p. 51) Elizabeth blushes with pleasure: 'I took great care.' The deceit is small, but even such a trivial hypocrisy may not be necessary in a well-balanced marital relationship; the consciousness of trying to please implies an unbalance which each is attempting to correct. Their actions and conversation show, in Miller's words, 'a sense of their separation' (p. 52), which has widened because of John's adultery with Abigail—an offence of extreme gravity in a puritan community.

This casts, as it were, a shadow over their relationship. Miller suggests this condition, when the couple speak together for the first time, by using the device of a seasonal metaphor. Although it is springtime, they live in a dark domesticity, symbolized by 'the low, dark, and rather long living-room' (p. 51) of the stage-setting. John has been out planting near the forest; now the farm is seeded. The implication made by associating farm with children is of a 'seeding' also in their marital relationship: 'Aye, the farm is seeded. The boys asleep?' As an audience learns later, Elizabeth is pregnant, and husband and wife now hope for a 'fair summer' which will make their farm and lives grow to fulfilment. John asserts in a moment of temporary optimism:

It's winter in here yet. On Sunday let you come with me, and we'll walk the farm together; I never see such a load of flowers on the earth. (p. 52)

But the 'wintry' shadow quickly falls again when there is mention of Abigail and the extension of her prestige in the village:

> She speak of Abigail, and I thought she were a saint, to hear her. Abigail brings the other girls into the court, and where she walks the crowd will part like the sea for Israel. (p. 53)

Ironically, John and Elizabeth (and an audience) know Abigail's appearance of saintliness and innocence contrasts with her sexual knowledge and desire to connive at Elizabeth's downfall.

In the unbalanced domestic situation the mere name of Abigail helps to separate husband and wife once more. John mentions that he was alone with her for a short time in Reverend Parris's house, and Elizabeth's suspicions are irrationally aroused. The atmosphere in the room changes from illusory optimism to suspicion and anger.

ELIZABETH: You were alone with her?

PROCTOR (*stubbornly*): For a moment alone, aye.

ELIZABETH: Why, then, it is not as you told me.

PROCTOR (*his anger rising*): For a moment, I say. The others come in soon after.

ELIZABETH (*quietly—she has suddenly lost all faith in him*): Do as you wish, then. (*She starts to turn.*)

PROCTOR: Woman. (*She turns to him.*) I'll not have your suspicion any more. . .

ELIZABETH: Then let you not earn it. (p. 54)

John's anger rises and, in an emotional torrent, charges

that she forgets nothing, forgives nothing and has little charity; he accuses her of being like a judge presiding in the court of their home. Elizabeth in reply insists, as she is to insist in the last meeting with her husband before his execution:

> I do not judge you. The magistrate sits in your heart that judges you. I never thought you but a good man, John—only somewhat bewildered. (p. 55)

She possesses a sharp psychological insight into his character. Aware that Abigail 'thinks to kill me, then to take my place' (p. 60), she warns her husband: 'You have a faulty understanding of young girls'—an observation which has been demonstrated by his encounter with Abigail in Act One and is to be further demonstrated by his treatment of Mary Warren.

In contrast to Abigail, who is characterized in part by her willingness to lie, the thought of deliberate lying is repugnant to Elizabeth, and one of the remarkably effective climaxes in Act Three is built upon this principle in her nature. During the trial, John states to Deputy Governor Danforth, 'That woman will never lie.' (p. 83) He repeats the assertion later:

> In her life, sir, she have never lied. There are them that cannot sing, and them that cannot weep—my wife cannot lie. (p. 98)

Then, in an effort to protect John's reputation, Elizabeth sacrifices the principle she holds most dear: she lies and, by the terrible irony of the situation, assists in the condemnation of her husband.

The period of physical separation and imprisonment, during which her pregnancy takes its course, effects a change in her. When she visits John before his execution, she refuses still to judge him, although she is confronted with a situation to which her fundamental principle is opposed. John, to save his life, considers the possibility of lying by signing a confession of his guilt. She is quietly resolute in the face of this possibility:

> It is not my soul, John, it is yours. Only be sure of this, for I know it now: Whatever you will do, it is a good man does it. (p. 119)

Perhaps her resolution has come from thinking upon John's 'goodness'; this, the confounding of her own principle in the courtroom, and the condition of pregnancy have induced her to read her heart. As a consequence, she has become aware of a past 'coldness' in her attitude to her husband.

As a girl she had thought herself so plain that she feared she might never marry; so deep had been this sense of inadequacy that, when John did offer her marriage, she was suspicious of him. It was this suspiciousness—a central trait in her character—underlying her 'coldness' which may have impelled her husband to seek the warm arms of Abigail. He is no 'wintry' man, and therefore could not be profoundly happy within a 'wintry' relationship. In cadenced prose, possessing the tautness of poetry, Elizabeth finally reveals to John with pathetic frankness this aspect of herself:

I counted myself so plain, so poorly made, no honest
love could come to me! Suspicion kissed you when I did;
I never knew how I should say my love. It were a cold
house I kept! . . . Forgive me, forgive me, John—I never
knew such goodness in the world! (p. 119)

Elizabeth has found a new deeper knowledge through
tribulation and a process of self-examining. Unjust accusation, her husband's imperilling himself to save her, her
own unintended condemnation of John, imprisonment and
pregnancy—have all contributed to this painful self-
knowledge; but most important, perhaps, in the social
dimensions of the drama, is the awareness, to one who
abominates lying, that consistent, reiterated and public
mendacity can compound disorder and make what is unnatural or evil seem morally right and just. Against this
reversal of values, a person can only seek and live by an
inner 'goodness'. With this discovery, Elizabeth's basic
insecurity—her wondering, feminine suspiciousness—is re-
duced: a profounder awareness replaces negative suspicion.
Like her husband in the final moments of his life, she has
her goodness now and no human force can take it away.

Extension projects:

(a) Reference has been made to the Introduction which
Arthur Miller has written to his *Collected Plays* (1957).
The ideas and arguments presented in this Introduction
provide a concise account of Miller's thinking about drama
and its relationship to society. In particular, those sections
referring to the composition of *The Crucible* should be
thoughtfully considered by a student of the play.
(b) It is sometimes helpful to clarify one's own perspective

on a work of art by comparing or contrasting it with another work which has some common features. A play that may profitably be read in conjunction with *The Crucible* is George Bernard Shaw's *St. Joan.* An obvious point of resemblance is that each contains a trial scene—some critics claiming that in *St. Joan* Shaw has written one of the most effective trial scenes in all drama. It might be interesting to begin one's comparison by studying the court proceedings presented in the two plays. Are there any similarities in the nature of the interrogation and the theocratic-political attitudes of the court officials?

Questions:

NOTE: Where references to the questions are given you might find further guidance to the play and a clearer understanding of the implications in the quotation by referring to the critical works themselves. This is not an essential procedure but one which is recommended.

1. By making detailed references to the text, construct your own arguments in *defence* of Abigail Williams.

2. 'Although Abigail has a few passionate lines as a jealous lover, she functions primarily as a catalyst in the intimidation-confession process.' (Leonard Moss, *Arthur Miller*, Twayne Publishers, Inc., 1967, p. 63.)

Define this statement in your own terms and demonstrate the extent of your agreement with it.

3. 'As a character Abigail shows no development.' How fully are you in accord with this comment?

4. 'Were it not for her power of life and death over many people, Abigail is a person to be pitied rather than condemned.' (C. J. Partridge) Discuss.

5. 'Elizabeth Proctor develops in the play to a self-aware and self-sacrificing adult; Abigail remains a selfish, passionate, and dangerous adolescent.' Discuss.

6. Make your own analysis of the marital relationship between John and Elizabeth Proctor

   (a) before Elizabeth is accused (Act Two)

   (b) after her appearance in court (Act Four).

7. 'Elizabeth continues to develop as a character during the last act.'

Clarify this statement by detailed analysis of Elizabeth's dialogue and function in Act Four.

8. 'Elizabeth, like St. Joan, has learnt through suffering that God's most precious gift is not life at any price, but the life of spiritual freedom and moral integrity.' (Dennis Welland, *Arthur Miller*, Oliver and Boyd, 1961, pp. 85–86) Discuss.

IV

A CONFLICT OF MEN: GILES COREY,
THOMAS PUTNAM, SAMUEL PARRIS,
DEPUTY GOVERNOR DANFORTH, JOHN HALE

'Great stones they lay upon his chest until he plead aye or nay. They say he give them but two words. "More weight," he says. And died.' (p. 118) Giles Corey was eighty-three years old when he met his death in the manner prescribed by English law. Because of his refusal to answer the charge of wizardry, even when 'pressed' by the stones, no official condemnation could be made. Thus his property was not legally confiscated—which was the additional punishment accorded those condemned on charges of witch-craft or wizardry. His sons were enabled to inherit because of the old man's silence. In a play where psychological and social ironies abound, Giles Corey's fate is one of the most savage of the dramatic ironies. A canny, inquisitive country-man, he is, like John Proctor, sturdily independent. He has cared little for public opinion (p. 43) and disregarded in-junctions to regular church attendance. Miller writes of him: 'He was a crank and a nuisance, but withal a deeply innocent and brave man.' (p. 43) He enjoys litigation and, from the dubious experience of having been in court pro-ceedings thirty-three times during his lifetime (p. 86), has learnt a great deal about legal process and terminology. It was doubtless on this knowledge that he drew when finally determining to keep silence and preserve his property.

But he was deeply resolved to prevent his land being

45

D

acquired through forfeiture by Thomas Putnam, and this may also have strengthened his silence. In the numerous squabbles over property his greatest enemy has been Thomas Putnam. If Corey was known locally as the litigious eccentric, Putnam was renowned for land rapacity.

His antagonism to Putnam and his independence of mind are shown during their early encounter in Reverend Parris's house. When discussion arises over the minister's salary and supply of firewood, Giles is initially opposed to Parris's complaints. He seems to side with John Proctor against the minister. When, however, the disagreement reaches a height of expressed anger, Giles refuses to join with Proctor in the latter's half-humorous wish to associate with the supposed anti-Parris faction:

> I've changed my opinion of this man, John. Mr. Parris, I beg your pardon. I never thought you had so much iron in you. (p. 35)

Then this litigious old man asks in a manner which makes the contrast between his own eccentricities and the serious question he raises have comic implications—'Wherefore is everybody suing everybody else? Think on it now, it's a deep thing, and dark as a pit.' (p. 36) Proctor sees the humour in the situation and responds accordingly, but the mood suddenly changes when Putnam intervenes with an assertion of property-rights. Recalling the man's famed rapacity for land, Giles is provoked to anger and, in his antagonism to Putnam, sides once again with John Proctor:

PUTNAM: You load one oak of mine and you'll fight to drag it home!

GILES: Aye, and we'll win too, Putnam—this fool and I.

(p. 36)

Despite the difference in age, Corey and Proctor are spiritually akin: their sense of independence makes them willing to confront any power which threatens that independence. Equally important is the fact that Giles suffers from an insecurity associated with guilt. Just as John can never forget his adultery with Abigail, so Giles cannot forget his mention of Martha reading books. During the first act, he had rambled on, in conversation with Reverend Hale, about his wife's reading:

I have waked at night many a time and found her in a corner, readin' of a book. . . It discomforts me! Last night—mark this—I tried and tried and could not say my prayers. And then she close her book and walks out of the house, and suddenly—mark this—I could pray again!

(p. 43)

Reverend Hale's solemn methodicalness had taken note of Martha Corey's literary interests and Giles' 'stoppage of prayer'; later, when she is to be condemned, among other charges, for the reading of *fortunes* (p. 78), Giles confronts the judges, thus attempting to defend his wife but also to alleviate his secret guilt. In broken phrases, uttered through sobs, he admits:

It is my third wife, sir; I never had no wife that be so taken with books, and I thought to find the cause of it, d'y'see, but it were no witch I blamed her for. (*He is openly weeping.*) (p. 79)

As John Proctor is slowly drawn into the centre of the judicial proceedings, the similarities between him and Corey become more evident. They had stood together against Putnam in Act One; they had felt bewildered and resentful at the accusations against their wives in Act Two; during the hearings they seek to defend the women and Corey again attacks Putnam—the man whose signature by this time appears on a number of official accusations—with the assertion that he is manipulating events for personal economic gain:

> If Jacobs hangs for a witch he forfeit up his property—that's law! And there is none but Putnam with the coin to buy so great a piece. This man is killing his neighbours for their land! (p. 87)

Unfortunately the only evidence Giles can offer to support this assertion is hearsay. He claims he was informed by a man who has heard Putnam say his purpose in signing accusations was judicial murder and acquisition of the victim's land. But when urged by Judge Hathorne to reveal the name of the informant who is thus implicating the much-respected Putnam, Giles is made rapidly aware of the trap-like power of the court:

HATHORNE: And the name of this man?
GILES (*taken aback*): What name?
HATHORNE: The man that give you this information.
GILES (*hesitates, then*): Why, I—I cannot give you his name.
HATHORNE: And why not?
GILES (*hesitates, then bursts out*): You know well why not!

He'll lay in jail if I give his name! . . . I will not give you no name. I mentioned my wife's name once and I'll burn in hell long enough for that. I stand mute.

DANFORTH: In that case, I have no choice but to arrest you for contempt of this court, do you know that? (p. 87)

The sturdy countryman Giles Corey anticipates the situation John Proctor is to endure: for him to reveal a name is to betray a loyalty, to hand his conscience, as on a plate, to a prejudiced interrogator. Revelation, especially under such a perversion of legal conditions, is destruction of a principle and, as is shown by his manner of dying, Giles Corey adheres fully to his principles. '"More weight," he says. And died. . . Aye. It were a fearsome man, Giles Corey.' (p. 118)

The similarities of temperament and tribulation shared by Corey and Proctor may be contrasted with the increasing identification of Putnam and Parris with the theocratic authorities. Each, as we have seen, has shown signs of psychological insecurity at the beginning of the drama but each grows more confirmed in his convictions as the prosecutions multiply. Putnam's accusations add to the hysteria; Reverend Parris's role becomes more overt, authoritarian and insidious.

When Proctor appears in court with Mary Warren it is Parris who, remembering the quarrel between himself and the farmer, warns: 'Beware this man, Your Excellency, this man is mischief.' (p. 80) He interposes again, shortly afterwards, with an almost hysterical fervour for which Judge Danforth obliquely rebukes him:

PARRIS: They've come to overthrow the court, sir! This man is—
DANFORTH: I pray you, Mr. Parris. (p. 81)

Undeterred, Reverend Parris insists that Proctor's attempt to discredit the evidence of Mary Warren and the other girls is the work of a disruptive, malevolent man whose Christian beliefs are not demonstrated by regular church attendance:

DANFORTH: You are in all respects a Gospel Christian?
PROCTOR: I am, sir.
PARRIS: Such a Christian that will not come to church but once in a month! (p. 82)

But even when allied with authority and convinced of his good standing with those who wield power, such a temperament as Parris possesses can never feel for long secure. After the hearings an attempt is made to assassinate him and the spread of civil disorder at the continuance of the witchcraft trials induces in him a state of panic. He informs Danforth, when they meet in Salem jail before the condemned are due to be hanged, of his fears that riot is spreading. In a gaunt, fevered condition, he advises postponement but, when his arguments based on preserving civil obedience do not affect Danforth's decision to continue with the executions, he describes the developing crisis in terms of personal danger:

Tonight, when I open my door to leave my house—a dagger clattered to the ground. You cannot hang this

sort. There is danger for me. I dare not step outside at
night! (p. 112)

His arguments have collapsed into non-logical assertions
stressing his own peril; such semi-coherent expostulations
have less effect on Danforth's steely resolution than his
previous cogency.

However, Reverend Parris survives while worthier men
are executed. He undergoes a type of purgation, moving
psychologically from uncertainty, to temporary identification with a perverse authority, to a final insecurity which is
worse than his first condition. The man of shifting personal
loyalties, without devotion to self-discovered principles,
disintegrates. Concerned with money and its slow accumu-
lation, he is finally robbed of his savings by Abigail (p. 111);
ironically, the young girl in whom he has placed so much
trust—both at home and in court—robs him not only of
money but also of trust in his own imprecise judgement.

Very different are the assured, ominous figures of Judge
Hathorne and Deputy Governor Danforth. Together they
occupy positions of power in 'the highest court of the
supreme government of this province' (p. 79). They embody
a mental attitude which, having consolidated that earlier
attitude by which metaphysical or theological explanations
stressing 'unnatural intervention' were provided as causes
for events, now acts inquisitorially within this fixed prejudiced framework. In the structure of *The Crucible* this
mentality and attitude was anticipated, as we have seen, in
the first act by Reverend Hale's method of interrogation.
In Act Two, spreading belief in the devil's presence and
the assertions of 'the afflicted girls' become accepted as

factual bases for making accusations against the villagers. In other words, when the court begins to conduct hearings, it does not question adequately the validity of the girls' evidence: instead, their testimony, no matter how absurd and unproven, is used as a basis for the interrogation of the accused. It is an attitude of mind on the part of the interrogators which contravenes legal impartiality and can only lead to conviction of the defendants. In dramatizing Hathorne's and Danforth's interrogation, Arthur Miller shows the mental rigidity by which such hearings in a time of community or national crisis may be conducted. In the words of the nineteenth-century historian C. W. Upham, during the Salem crisis the examination of more than one defendant

> was conducted in the form of questions put by the magistrate, Hathorne, based upon a foregone conclusion of the prisoner's guilt, and expressive of a conviction . . . that the evidence of 'the afflicted' against her amounted to, and was, absolute demonstration.
>
> *(Salem Witchcraft*, p. 16)

The clearest dramatized portrayals of this attitude pervading the courtroom are given by Hathorne and Danforth. Of the two, the more rounded characterization in the play is that of Danforth. A highly intelligent man, trained in the manner of a lawyer to make sharp rational distinctions, he nevertheless accepts with insufficient questioning the evidence of 'the afflicted'. At one point he warns Proctor:

> I tell you straight, Mister—I have seen marvels in this court. I have seen people choked before my eyes by

spirits; I have seen them stuck by pins and slashed by daggers. I have until this moment not the slightest reason to suspect that the children may be deceiving me. (p. 83)

The contrast between his undoubted intelligence and these assertions of supernatural causes is startling to an audience. It is as though a plough has torn through the subtle mental discriminations of which he is capable; on either side of the unbridgeable furrow is an inviolable category. On the one hand, God's order, which is the existing condition of things, must be preserved; on the other, the 'unnatural' sickness of children and deaths of animals are consequences of an intrigue to undermine the social order. No man can shelter within the furrow and those who intrigue must be found, brought to the side of God—or else exterminated. Fixed in these convictions, he is not amenable to returning to greater subtlety of thought, even when need for this is implied by Reverend Hale:

HALE: There is a prodigious fear of this court in the country—

DANFORTH: Then there is a prodigious guilt in the country. Are *you* afraid to be questioned here?

HALE: I may only fear the Lord, sir, but there is fear in the country nevertheless.

DANFORTH (*angered now*): Reproach me not with the fear in the country; there is fear in the country because there is a moving plot to topple Christ in the country! (p. 88)

The repetition of the phrase 'fear in the country' suggests the developing hysteria; that it may spread like a disease through the community is of little significance to Danforth;

his essential purpose is to separate the community into two groups—those who are on the side of God and those who are not. He has stated explicitly to Francis Nurse:

> A person is either with this court or he must be counted against it, there be no road between. This is a sharp time, now, a precise time—we live no longer in the dusky afternoon when evil mixed itself with good and befuddled the world. Now, by God's grace, the shining sun is up, and them that fear not light will surely praise it.   (p. 85)

One may question the nature of the sun to which Deputy Governor Danforth refers. In the stage settings for the four acts, the sun is always exterior and only a small part of its light illumines the rooms, courthouses and prison of Salem. The sun referred to in Danforth's asseveration is largely in his own mind—a subjective sun of burning consolidated delusion directed as a death-force against those he believes inimical to the social order.

Essentially this force derives from his simplistic categorizing; psychologically such intellectual simplicity increases the rigid quality of a mind. Having determined on which side a person is—whether God's or the devil's—it becomes difficult to retain a mental alertness so that evidence may be re-examined and new decisions made. Such rigidity is, of course, a fatal defect in one who administers justice; its dominance in the minds of Hathorne and Danforth is demonstrated by their biased cross-examination:

DANFORTH (*turning to Abigail*): A poppet were discovered in Mr. Proctor's house, stabbed by a needle. . . While you worked for Mr. Proctor, did you see poppets in that house?

ABIGAIL: Goody Proctor always kept poppets.

PROCTOR: Your Honour, my wife never kept no poppets. Mary Warren confesses it was her poppet. . .

CHEEVER: When I spoke with Goody Proctor in that house, she said she never kept no poppets. But she said she did keep poppets when she were a girl.

PROCTOR: She has not been a girl these fifteen years, Your Honour.

HATHORNE: But a poppet will keep fifteen years, will it not?
(pp. 92–93)

The incident further dramatizes the inability of the judges to conceive of falsity in the testimony of 'the afflicted girls.' That Abigail may be anxious to plot Elizabeth's death by the absurd device of placing a needle in the stomach of a doll, or that Mary Warren may have been deluded in seeing spirits active in the courtroom is not deeply entertained as a possibility. Francis Nurse had exclaimed at the beginning of the proceedings: 'Excellency, we have proof for your eyes; God forbid you shut them to it.' (p. 79) Unfortunately, this proof for the eyes, this evidence of the senses, this employment of plain common sense is not acceptable to men of large mental rigidity. Too easily delusion becomes fanaticism among people 'so fanatically wedded to orthodoxy that they could not cope with the evidence of their senses.' (Arthur Miller, *The Saturday Review*, 31 January, 1953.)

Luckless Mary Warren with her 'peeping courage' hovers between the opposing sides, represented by Corey and Proctor on the one hand, and the court officials on the other. So also does Reverend John Hale. Neither he nor

Mary Warren has the resourcefulness to maintain a personal conscience about the course of events and hence are victims of moral indetermination. The more pathetic case is that of Reverend Hale.

We have seen him in Act One present a ludicrous seriousness and naïve dogmatism, but this intellectual and professional certainty does not remain with him; his intellectual edifice partly crumbles through the tragic force of events. When he enters John Proctor's house in the following act he is slightly changed—'there is a quality of deference, even of guilt, about his manner now' (p. 61). He has come on his own initiative (thus anticipating his voluntary visit to Salem jail in Act Four) possibly to warn John that his wife's name has been mentioned in court. He admits that he now has difficulty in drawing 'a clear opinion' about the growing numbers of the accused; already a lack of intellectual clarity is replacing that dogmatic certitude which *precisely* categorized the existence and movements of spirits. However, at this time, he possesses only a small uncertainty for he re-states his dogmatic belief to the Proctors:

No man may longer doubt the powers of the dark are gathered in monstrous attack upon this village. There is too much evidence now to deny it. . . Theology, sir, is a fortress; no crack in a fortress may be accounted small.
(p. 62, p. 65)

But the fortress, like his intellectual edifice, is to show some cracks as the proceedings in court, during Act Three, resume.

By the time of the court hearings four hundred people

are imprisoned and seventy-two have been condemned to death. Hale has affixed his signature to the death-warrants (p. 89) and the remarkably large number of witches that have been discovered among a relatively small population causes him some bewilderment. As he witnesses the cross-examination of Elizabeth Proctor, further doubts assail him. At the end of her testimony, when by lying she has condemned her husband, Hale exclaims:

> Excellency, it is a natural lie to tell; I beg you, stop now before another is condemned! I may shut my conscience to it no more—private vengeance is working. . . (p. 100)

He is convinced of John Proctor's truthfulness, distrusts the evidence of Abigail (p. 100), but sees her trickery and 'private vengeance' prevailing. With John Proctor he denounces the proceedings and rushes from the court, slamming the door behind him (p. 105).

They are the gestures of a weak man. His early assurance gone, he is no longer able to identify with the moral rightness of official orthodoxy. The final encounter between Danforth and Hale reveals the immovable rigidity of the former and the new, anxious self-questioning of the minister. In the jail, Danforth is somewhat suspicious of him:

> What is he about here? . . . That man have no authority to enter here, Marshal.   (p. 109)

Hale, having relinquished all official association with the court, tries now to act on the promptings of his emergent conscience; when Danforth coldly congratulates him on ministering to the condemned, Hale's blunt response is:

'You must pardon them.' (p. 113) But the Deputy Governor has become a rigid mechanism irrevocably confirmed in the moral rightness of his decision-making: he embodies the power enacting God's law:

> While I speak God's law, I will not crack its voice with whimpering. If retaliation is your fear, know this—I should hang ten thousand that dared to rise against the law, and an ocean of salt tears could not melt the resolution of the statutes. (p. 113)

Against this, Reverend Hale—the man caught between his own newly-questioning mind and fixed moral orthodoxy—cries self-pityingly:

> I come to do the Devil's work. . . There is blood on my head! Can you not see the blood on my head!! (p. 114)

When he speaks to Elizabeth he urges her to persuade her husband to adopt a similarly compromising and self-pitying position; a false confession will save John's life. But, ironically, he is addressing a woman to whom lying is abhorrent. With a further subtle dramatic irony, rejecting the advice of the one person who at last sees the magnitude of terror and social disorder around them, she quietly says: 'I think that be the Devil's argument.' (p. 115)

Hale is a very different man from the one presented in the opening acts of the play. Then, convinced equally of legal justice and of a plot against the natural civil order of Salem, he had asserted on learning of saintly Rebecca Nurse's arrest:

If Rebecca Nurse be tainted, then nothing's left to stop the whole green world from burning. Let you rest upon the justice of the court. . . I have seen too many frightful proofs in court—the Devil is alive in Salem, and we dare not quail to follow wherever the accusing finger points!
(pp. 67–68)

He has followed the accusing finger and found that, under the delusive, hysteria-inducing sun, a green world of innocence is capable of burning. Recoiling finally from the perversion of human values that has resulted, he has not been able to find any personal satisfying compromise. The final image is of a once-resolute man now become irresolute and victim of a disorder he had, with initial good faith, helped to foster. Kneeling in the jail, he pathetically asks of Elizabeth:

What profit him to bleed? Shall the dust praise him? Shall the worms declare his truth? Go to him, take his shame away!
(pp. 125–126)

She prefers that John die with this 'shame' because, by the values of a private conscience more developed than that possessed by Reverend Hale, such dying is a form of glory.

Extension project:

Arthur Miller has made a recording in which he comments on, and reads from, *The Crucible* and *Death of a Salesman*. Further understanding of *The Crucible* may be assisted by listening to the dramatist's introductory remarks and his manner of reading extracts from Act Two.

Arthur Miller: *The Crucible, Death of a Salesman*, Spoken Arts, Inc., Distinguished Playwright Series, No. 704.

Questions:

1. Arthur Miller refers to Giles Corey as 'the most comical hero' in the history of the events at Salem. What elements of comedy do you find in his presentation of Corey?

2. Write a *defence* of Deputy Governor Danforth's attitude and activities.

3. Define the nature of rigidity in Deputy Governor Danforth.

4. Contrast the self-assurance and role of Reverend Hale in Acts One and Two with his self-questioning and role in the concluding acts.

5. Outline the moral growth of John Hale.

6. 'The characters in *The Crucible* may be described as either maturing or ethically fixed personalities.' (Leonard Moss, *Arthur Miller*, Twayne Publishers, Inc., 1967, p. 63.)

   Define this statement in your own terms and apply your definition to a discussion of at least three characters.

7. It has been frequently assumed by critics that the subsidiary figures in *The Crucible* are static—that is, they are not developed as 'rounded characters' by the dramatist. To what extent do you agree with the critics' assumption?

8. 'In terms of sustained conflict, Acts Two and Three are the most dramatic. These middle acts focus on thrust and counter-thrust, and the tension is generally high.' (Edward Murray, *Arthur Miller, Dramatist*, Frederick Ungar Publishing Co., 1967, p. 60.)

   Define these statements in your own terms, illustrating your definition by discussion of particular encounters between characters in the two acts.

9. '*The Crucible* explores two contrary processes in the context of a given social order—the generation of hysteria and the achievement of moral honesty.' (Leonard Moss, *Arthur Miller*, Twayne Publishers, Inc., 1967, p. 64.)

Discuss this comment by *detailed* analysis of particular encounters between characters in Acts Three and Four.

10. 'The very considerable dramatic power of *The Crucible* derives from its revelation of a mounting tide of evil gaining, in an entire society, an ascendancy quite disproportionate to the evil of any individual member of that society.' (Dennis Welland, *Arthur Miller*, Oliver and Boyd, 1961, p. 84).)

Discuss.

E

V

TRAGEDY AND THE COMMON MAN: JOHN PROCTOR

In 1949, the year he achieved great success with the production of *Death of a Salesman* in New York, Arthur Miller attempted to re-define the nature of tragedy. In an article written for *The New York Times* called 'Tragedy and the Common Man',[1] he argued against the traditional association in western drama of tragic downfall with the figure of a king or nobleman. He saw this emphasis on social rank as unnecessary for the writing of modern tragedy.

In the nineteenth century the Norwegian dramatist Henrik Ibsen had shown in such plays as *An Enemy of the People* (1882), *Rosmersholm* (1886) and *John Gabriel Borkman* (1896) that tragedy could be conceived around the lives of professional middle-class men and women; the influence of Ibsen on Miller's thinking and dramatic expression has been profound and pervasive. In his article, the American playwright argues that tragedy today may dramatize the predicament of a common man—'I believe that the common man is as apt a subject for tragedy in its highest sense as kings were.' He may be a struggling salesman, such as Willy Loman in *Death of a Salesman*, or an

[1] This important article first appeared in *The New York Times*, 27 February, 1949, II, p. 1, p. 3. It may be most readily available in Gerald Weales's critical edition of *Death of a Salesman*, The Viking Press, 1967, pp. 143–47.

ordinary farmer like John Proctor in *The Crucible*. What is central to Miller's concept of a modern tragic protagonist is stated in these terms:

> The tragic feeling is evoked in us when we are in the presence of a character who is ready to lay down his life, if need be, to secure one thing—his sense of personal dignity. From Orestes to Hamlet, Medea to Macbeth, the underlying struggle is that of the individual attempting to gain his 'rightful' position in his society.
>
> Sometimes he is one who has been displaced from it, sometimes one who seeks to attain it for the first time, but the fateful wound from which the inevitable events spiral is the wound of indignity, and its dominant force is indignation. Tragedy, then, is the consequence of a man's total compulsion to evaluate himself justly.

To be wounded by indignity, filled with growing indignation and to struggle in securing a personal dignity is John Proctor's experience. However, *The Crucible* achieves considerable complexity, as we have seen, when the hero's effort to gain his 'rightful' position is in a society where, because of fanatical devotion to an orthodoxy, human values have become perverted.

If the protagonist were willing to submit—that is, accept the indignity imposed upon him—he could survive as a man-in-the-street without tragic significance. But, instead, he protests, refusing conformity to the forces surrounding him. In other words, he discovers—painfully, through experience—an individual course of action; he commits himself to this, and does so with such intensity that violence is unleashed against him. This sequence of events, central to tragedy, may be expressed in Miller's own words:

> I see the process, essentially as this: the hero is one, unlike most men, who quite unknowingly or with a certain degree of foreknowledge, *acts* at a moment when others would go silent or retire. In so acting he causes the scheme of things to react with retributive violence against him. It is a question of pressing the mechanism beyond its ability to exist in quiet. At bottom it is a questing after knowledge, a knowledge which is forbidden. . . His 'fault' is that he lacks wisdom—he cannot let well enough alone, he cannot respect danger sufficiently.
> (Sheila Huftel, *Arthur Miller: The Burning Glass*, The Citadel Press, 1965, p. 113)

The extent to which these definitions of tragic action characterize John Proctor should be obvious. His intensity of commitment varies through the drama, as does the retributive violence inflicted on him. His questing after knowledge is a process of mind—a fluidity opposed to the rigidity of accusers and prosecutors—by which a degree of self-knowledge and integrity is ultimately found. Thus, the common farmer attains tragic status by his questioning of values to secure the dignity of a private, innerly-satisfying conscience. Miller writes in the introduction to his *Collected Plays*:

> It matters not at all whether a modern play concerns itself with a grocer or a president if the intensity of the hero's commitment to his course is less than the maximum possible. It matters not at all whether the hero

falls from a great height or a small one, whether he is highly conscious or only dimly aware of what is happening, whether his pride brings the fall or an unseen pattern written behind clouds; if the intensity, the human passion to surpass his given bounds . . . if these are not present there can only be an outline of tragedy but no living thing.   (*Collected Plays*, p. 33)

The bounds which are to be surpassed in the community of Salem become fixed with terror. To trespass beyond the newly-imposed conformities may bring denunciation and death. The bounds are embodied in the figure of Danforth who, as we have seen, promotes public fear in the name of justice and destroys human life with the self-imagined approval of God. Danforth, as Deputy Governor, prosecutor and judge, may represent 'the power of theocracy in Massachusetts' (p. 127), but is also essentially the figure who imposes limitations on others. Beyond these no man may trespass without peril. In different societies, both past and present, boundaries may take the form of élite rule, or limitations by class, or exclusive control of governmental and educational systems; no matter how they are made real, such a man as Danforth must appear to preserve the existing state of things and to punish those who question them. Miller has commented on this symbolic aspect of Danforth's function:

Danforth was indeed dedicated to securing the status quo against such as Proctor. But I am equally interested in his *function* in the drama, which is that of the rule-bearer, the man who always guards the boundaries which, if you insist on breaking through them, have the power to destroy you. His 'evil' is more than personal, it is nearly mythical. He does more evil than he knows how to do; while merely following his nose he guards ignorance, he is man's limit.

(Sheila Huftel, *Arthur Miller: The Burning Glass*, p. 146)

Against this limit Proctor ventures, sometimes with indignation, sometimes with deliberate intent. His struggle is to make a private conscience when public sins are being invented daily and the mechanism of state urges confession based on the new sins. His progression is from a common sense wounded by this environment, through greater self-knowledge, towards a just, moral evaluation of himself.

As is the fate with many of Ibsen's protagonists, Miller's heroes can never fully escape the consequences of a deed performed in the past. Although they may have suffered in conscience for an earlier failing, it returns under the exigencies of a present crisis to hurt them with renewed force. John Proctor's adultery with Abigail has been committed 'where my beasts are bedded' (p. 97) some eight months previous to the trials. In his wife's opinion John has 'a faulty understanding of young girls' (p. 60) and, in his later view of the relationship, it is seen as no more than a physical beast-like act—'The promise that a stallion gives a mare I gave that girl!' (p. 61) But such an assertion cannot dismiss an abiding awareness of guilt. It is implied by his description of the act in animal images—upright puritan man has been relegated by his lust to the level of a beast; it is also inferred by the atmosphere of separation between John and Elizabeth conveyed by the actions and dialogue at the beginning of Act Two. Behind the surface of their conversation lies a friction which has disrupted the harmony of the home.

When, however, John by the course of events is forced to choose between his wife and Abigail, marital loyalty prevails. Although he is at first unwilling to proclaim publicly that Abigail is perpetrating a fraud by her imputations of witchcraft, his instinct towards defence of Elizabeth, by ripping the Deputy Governor's warrant, demonstrates the area of his profounder loyalty. His wife's fears that Abigail wishes her death become clear to John at this moment. He realizes that 'vengeance is walking Salem' (p. 72), that behind the social purge which is taking place private hatreds and personal antagonisms contribute largely to the accusers' motivations. A sense of his individual aloneness afflicts him after the departure of Elizabeth in chains. He exclaims:

> Now Hell and Heaven grapple on our backs, and all our old pretence is ripped away. . . We are only what we always were, but naked now. Aye, naked! And the wind, God's icy wind, will blow! (pp. 74–75)

The pretence of loving Abigail has been dispersed: in the implied comparison, the sexual grapplings of beast-like lust are not now the dominant reality; instead, there is a naked aloneness in which more powerful forces operate blowing, like God's icy wind, through the remnants of individual pretence.

An assertiveness, far deeper than secret guilt, has always characterized Proctor. Even the relationship with Abigail, against the law of his religion and community, required a daring insistence. A man in his mid-thirties, he is a formidable figure in whose presence 'a fool felt his foolishness.'

(p. 27) So, apparently, was the historical John Proctor. In the sketch made of him by the nineteenth-century historian C. W. Upham the individual manliness of his character is stressed:

> He was a person of decided character, and, although impulsive and liable to be imprudent, of a manly spirit, honest, earnest, and bold in word and deed. He saw through the whole thing, and was convinced that it was the result of a conspiracy, deliberate and criminal, on the part of the accusers. He gave free utterance to his indignation at their conduct, and it cost him his life.
>
> (*Salem Witchcraft*, p. 304)

This individual manliness, or inner integrity, is conveyed during Act One by the dramatized encounters with Reverend Parris and Thomas Putnam. The common sense of this common man is revealed in contrast to Parris's growing hysteria, when the latter tells of his summoning Reverend Hale:

PARRIS: A wide opinion's running in the parish that the Devil may be among us, and I would satisfy them that they are wrong.

PROCTOR: Then let you come out and call them wrong. Did you consult the wardens before you called this minister to look for devils?

PARRIS: He is not coming to look for devils!

PROCTOR: Then what's he coming for?

PUTNAM: There be children dyin' in the village, Mister!

PROCTOR: I seen none dyin'. This society will not be a bag to swing around your head, Mr. Putnam. (pp. 32–33)

He shows a sharply intuitive awareness that Putnam's anxiety about his child may be part of the man's obsession to extend his social power. He is suspicious of the authoritarian tendencies in each, as both Parris and Putnam have acted without consulting other members of the community. His somewhat contemptuous attitude towards Parris—'I like not the smell of this "authority"' (p. 35)—and his rebuke to Putnam—'We vote by name in this society, not by acreage' (p. 33)—suggest a man who has *convictions* but has not yet experienced sufficient adversity to realize the depth of his *principles*.

The adversity is not long in coming. Proctor becomes a divided man simultaneously separate from his wife, victim of intrigue by a woman with whom he has had extramarital carnal relations, and wounded by a legal procedure which, based on common law, now acts against common men and common sense. The ensuing struggle to retain his individual manliness contributes to a deepening self-knowledge; a need to preserve his 'name'—his private conscience, his inner integrity, his relatedness to what he conceives to be truth—impels him by word and deed towards an effort at self-evaluation.

Proctor's struggle through Act Three is partly against the rigidified, perverted mentality of the accusers, and partly to overcome his own fears of 'nakedness'. The fears are large because of the guilt remaining from his adultery. The innate assertiveness of his nature gains him the privilege of making a deposition—after reiterating that his purpose is not to overthrow the court. His pleadings with Mary Warren have been effective in persuading this girl of 'peeping courage' to rescind her previous testimony. The conflict is then between himself and Abigail as they 'grapple' in the courtroom; when it seems that she and her pretences will prevail and Mary Warren is almost collapsing from the other girls' intimidation, Proctor leaps towards Abigail, the leader of 'the afflicted girls', grabbing her by the hair and calling her a whore. With this, he is forced to avow his past relationship with her, and stand publicly as a guilty fornicator.

Now, for John Proctor, the fearful ironies multiply: confession of his private conscience is not accepted by the court, although denunciations by the girls are still regarded as valid; the wife, whose truthfulness he has never before had reason to doubt, lies to save him and, in effect, discredits his testimony; Abigail gains further power in the courtroom by leading the other girls against Mary Warren, and terrifying her, so that she ultimately denounces Proctor: 'You're the Devil's man!' (p. 104)

In his struggle against the bounds of a hysteria-supported orthodoxy Proctor has lost all. Having overcome a reluctance to involve himself in the proceedings and to act against Abigail, he has done so to save his wife and plead for the lives of others. He can gain justice only by involvement in the legal process; but, by becoming involved, he transgresses certain boundaries and is then one of the accused. His effort at securing justice is thwarted in the name of justice.

By suffering the absurdity and terror of this experience, Proctor grows aware of a developing sense of social responsibility. Human values have been so perverted during the hearing and trial that he cannot see God guiding the court officials in promoting further distortions of justice; in Proctor's view, the proceedings are rather the devil's instrument for instilling fear in innocent people. Consequently, in the climax to Act Three, he denies the existence of a God such as Danforth imagines is guiding his absolute moral rightness. By announcing the death of God, Proctor is attacking that rigid, simplistic absolutism, tantamount to superstition, which asserts that there can be 'no road between' (p. 85) absolute opposites. An intuition of the social need to lead men from such ignorance of imposed superstition is expressed in his last, defiant words to the court:

> I hear the boot of Lucifer, I see his filthy face! And it is my face, and yours, Danforth! For them that quail to bring men out of ignorance, as I have quailed, and as you quail now when you know in all your black hearts that this be fraud—God dams our kind especially, and we will burn, we will burn together! . . . You are pulling Heaven down and raising up a whore!   (p. 105)

After experiencing such cumulative absurdities and ironies of justice, John Proctor has grown conscious of a social responsibility. His initial reluctant involvement has given way to forthright condemnation of rule-bearers and boundary-makers such as Danforth who may use mass ignorance, superstition, prejudice and hysteria to consolidate their power in the society over which they rule.

After months of imprisonment Proctor is transformed. He is no longer that formidable figure, 'powerful of body' (p. 27), in whose presence Abigail had stood 'wide-eyed' (p. 28) and her friend Mercy Lewis had felt 'strangely titillated' (p. 28). Autumn has replaced springtime; his walk is slow, his wrists are chained, he is 'bearded, filthy, his eyes misty as though webs had overgrown them' (p. 116). But when his wife meets him in Salem jail there is no longer any feeling of separation between them; their conversation has a simple directness which contrasts with the hidden friction of their first appearance together at the beginning of Act Two. Suffering has effected a deeper understanding between husband and wife; in John Proctor there is also a deeper understanding of himself.

The quiet, understated dialogue conveys a richness of emotion, born of suffering, beyond mere words:

PROCTOR: The child?
ELIZABETH: It grows.
PROCTOR: There is no word of the boys?
ELIZABETH: They're well. Rebecca's Samuel keeps them.
PROCTOR: You have not seen them?
ELIZABETH: I have not.
PROCTOR: You are a—marvel, Elizabeth.
ELIZABETH: You—have been tortured?
PROCTOR: Aye. They come for my life now.   (p. 117)

He has half-resolved that he will submit to the perverse authoritarian pressures which commit evil in the name of goodness, justice and God. Perhaps his intention is provoked by a momentary, but profound, fear which afflicts him on learning of Giles Corey's agonizing death; more importantly, however, these months of self-examination in prison have not convinced him that he is a 'good man' (p. 118), so that to appear as a martyr for his own cause would be fraudulent and pretentious. He asserts: 'Spite only keeps me silent. It is hard to give a lie to dogs.' (pp. 118–119)

Elizabeth, knowing her husband's independence of mind, quietly insists he make his own uninfluenced decision and assures him of his 'goodness': 'Whatever you will do, it is a good man does it.' (p. 119) Her words both strengthen and dismay him. He is given the responsibility of evaluating himself and his actions when she says: 'But let none be your judge. There be no higher judge under Heaven than Proctor is!' (p. 119)

The essential agony of his divided mind is dramatized in the last encounters of the play with the rule-bearers, Hathorne and Danforth. He appears to submit to their demarcated orthodoxy knowing that he must lie in order to live and conscious also that, although Elizabeth wants him to live, a lie is abhorrent to her. Passively, before the direct questioning of the interrogators, he admits complicity with the devil:

DANFORTH: Did you see the Devil?
PROCTOR: I did. . .
DANFORTH: And when he come to you, what were his
    demand? Did he bid you to do his work upon the earth?
PROCTOR: He did.
DANFORTH: And you bound yourself to his service? . . .
    Did you bind yourself to the Devil's service? . . .
PROCTOR: I did.   (p. 121)

With similar passivity he replies to questions about neighbours and friends, denying their complicity; but, in the course of this cross-examination, a sullen resentment is growing in him. The saintly, but condemned, Rebecca Nurse is present and, when urged repeatedly, to implicate her, Proctor cries out with hatred in his voice: 'I speak my

own sins; I cannot judge another. I have no tongue for it.'
(p. 123) For those who know the biographical details of
Arthur Miller's personal conflict with moral orthodoxy
there is an echo, in John Proctor's defiant refusal, of
Miller's own assertion: 'I take responsibility for everything I have ever done, but I cannot take responsibility for
another human being.'

Slowly Proctor's attitude of individualistic protest re-
forms. He signs a confession, as is demanded of him. But
then, hatred turning to anger and terror (p. 123), he snatches
at the signed document. Deputy Governor Danforth is per-
plexed, but polite and controlled at first:

DANFORTH: Mr. Proctor, I must have good and legal proof
that you—
PROCTOR: Tell them I confessed myself.   (p. 124)

The distinction Proctor makes is between a private conscience, admitting its doubts to God, and the public manipulation of such a confession by a rigid establishment,
absolutist in its inviolable rightness. Proctor has felt a
psychological need to admit his doubts and self-deprecia-
tions; but then to be made the subject of manipulation by
a coercive dogmatism arouses the 'protestant' in him. He
realizes to the full the consequences for a 'protestant' and
a society when 'a political policy is equated with moral
right, and opposition to it with diabolical malevolence.'
(See Chapter One.)

At last, in this final confrontation, he is able to evaluate
himself justly. Distraught, 'weeping in fury' (p. 125), he
tears and crumples the confession and is capable of recog-
nizing his inner integrity: 'Now I do think I see some shred

of goodness in John Proctor. Not enough to weave a banner with, but white enough to keep it from such dogs.' (p. 125) His fear of appearing a fraud or pretender have departed and the passive victim has become again a figure of positive assertiveness; he is more dignified now in his own mind because distress, unjust accusation, physical and mental torture have confirmed him in his principle of 'goodness'. Elizabeth remains when her husband with Rebecca Nurse —the saintly embodiment of common sense—is led to execution. A reference to eating had characterized Rebecca's first utterances in Act One (p. 32), and it also characterizes her final exit; as she is taken to death, with a touch of comic pathos, she murmurs: 'I've had no breakfast' (p. 125). After their departure, Elizabeth cries aloud, reiterating John's, and her, new-found faith: 'He have his goodness now.' (p. 126)

In a drama which deals with mass hysteria and collective terror these forces predominate, and principles of rationality and humaneness seem subsidiary. Despite this, the final impression conveyed by *The Crucible* is not one of hopeless pessimism. Perhaps it is no more than a suspicion, perhaps a small conviction, that individual integrity can survive amid imposed conformity which a spectator takes with him from a performance. Sometimes it is a generalized sensation that, in the face of oppression, man will not only endure but also prevail.

Part of the satisfying effect produced by the play derives, as in most significant works of art, from its author's control of form. The manner in which Miller has shaped the complex psychological and social material reveals the hand of a sure craftsman. Beneath the action, conflicts and development of characters, a secure structure may be discerned. It is essentially the same in each act and contributes to the changes of atmosphere and alterations of tempo which any producer staging the play must carefully study. This basic structure may be schematized in the following manner:

(a) a posture of defensiveness
(b) interrogation (active questioning)
(c) impetus to forced confession
(d) confessional (partly hysterical) outburst

Each act begins with a posture of defensiveness by the characters present on stage; thus, at the beginning of Act One, Reverend Parris is fearful of his daughter's sickness and the invasions of some disorder into his household and parish; at the beginning of Act Two, John Proctor is defensive, because of his past adultery, in the presence of his wife; in Act Three, Martha Corey is proclaiming her innocence to Judge Hathorne; in Act Four, Sarah Good and Tituba seek consolation in drink and extravagant talk before their execution.

Each act dramatizes at least one sequence of interrogation—for instance, by Reverends Parris and Hale in Acts One and Two, by Hathorne and Danforth in Acts Three and Four. The questioners' purpose is to force a confession, which Abigail provides in the first scene and Proctor, with varying degrees of self-knowledge, in the following scenes.

The climax of each act is a confessional, sometimes hysterical, outburst: Abigail and 'the afflicted girls' chant and gyrate on the stage to implicate people for conspiring with the devil in Acts One and Three; John Proctor, at the conclusion of Acts Two, Three and Four makes large emotional statements against pretence in both victims and accusers. In the final scene his profoundest confessional outburst is followed, as we have noted, by Elizabeth's quiet reiteration of faith in his integrity so that the conclusion to the drama demonstrates Miller's view on the central purpose of tragedy:

> If it is true to say that in essence the tragic hero is intent upon claiming his whole due as a personality, and if this struggle must be total and without reservation, then it automatically demonstrates the indestructible will of man to achieve his humanity. . . It is curious, although edifying, that the plays we revere, century after century, are the tragedies. In them, and in them alone, lies the belief—optimistic, if you will, in the perfectibility of man.   ('Tragedy and the Common Man')

Some awareness of the dramatic craft he has employed to achieve this optimistic response in a spectator may be gained by more detailed personal analysis of the basic structure.

However, neither optimism nor structure were perceptible to audiences and critics when *The Crucible* was first performed in New York in 1953. Amid that period's atmosphere of suspicion and intrigue, the response of theatre critics was abrupt, pessimistic and, for the most part, antagonistic.

Often, political prejudice was revealed by the published comments of reviewers and newspapers. Miller was attacked for displaying a distressing note of stridency through his obsessive ideological preoccupations. A left-wing journal, *Masses and Mainstream*, praised these ideological concerns

F

and saw *The Crucible* as 'a positive contribution to the fight against McCarthyism'; the internationally distributed conservative magazine, *Time*, tore against bounds of language and syntax to deliver a largely incoherent diatribe:

> The play is curiously unmoving; while its foreground story is even without sociological relevancy. Turning on a slut's purely malicious lie. (*Time*, 2 February, 1953)

A more distinguished dramatic commentator, for elegant phrases and critical impercipience, admonished the playwright for creating a mechanical parable:

> For Salem, and the people who live, love, fear and die in it, are really only conveniences to Mr. Miller, props to his thesis. He does not make them interesting in and for themselves, and you wind up analysing them, checking their dilemmas against the latest headlines, rather than losing yourself in any rounded, deeply rewarding personalities.
>
> (Walter F. Kerr, *New York Herald Tribune*,
> 23 January, 1953)

More perceptive critics have seen the implications of the play reverberating far beyond immediate social issues. Their arguments on its universal, tragic significance have usually emphasized two aspects: first, they have seen as central the relationship between John and Elizabeth and the quality of self-developing awareness in each; secondly, defenders of the work have emphasized its conflict as a struggle with incarnate evil. That this evil has contemporary or historical parallels was less important than the fact that some monstrous power could be released with destructive force. The major question raised in *The Crucible*, according to one academic commentator, is 'How should a man act in the face of evil?' (Edward Murray, *Arthur Miller, Dramatist*, Frederick Ungar Publishing Co., 1967, pp. 52–75.)

Producers of the play, like academic critics, may also stress different aspects of the work. *The Crucible* may be staged in the manner of a naturalistic drama so that the audience 'looks in', as it were, on an appearance of real life in private homes, courthouse and prison cell. The heightened language of the dialogue, tending frequently to a prose-poetry, may be declaimed to convey a sense of historical authenticity although, in the utterances of inexperienced actors, it can appear as facile rhetoric. Thus a naturalistic production may suggest the appearance of historical reality while implying the relevance of the moral crisis in Salem society to all times and all places.

Alternatively, it is possible to present *The Crucible* in a manner the German dramatist Bertolt Brecht might have preferred. Instead of an audience 'looking in' on events which are separate from them by naturalistic staging and appearances of historical authenticity, a producer might employ devices to involve spectators in the action. One such device is to excerpt passages from the prose commentary which Miller inserts in the text; an actor, directly addressing the audience, states these additional views of the playwright on seventeenth-century theocratic society, the strange occurrences in Salem and the psychological complexity of the central characters. Another device promoting audience participation is to have the court officials wear modern dress—not the robes of an impartial judge but the more sinister dark suits a contemporary spectator might associate with secret police in authoritarian countries where active dissent is discouraged. The difference between this garb and the historical dress of the accused may provoke in an audience the thought: 'This could happen to us, and it is happening *now* in some part of the world.' Thirdly, this Brechtian manner of dramatizing the problems of relatedness and responsibility between an individual and the society around him may end with a direct address to the audience using the words of Miller's final commentary.

In this we are informed that Reverend Parris departed from Salem and disappeared never to be heard of again. Abigail, taking Parris's money, also disappeared and legend suggests she became a prostitute in Boston. The land belonging to the victims was regarded as having a curse upon it; farms were left to ruin and remained untenanted for more than a century. Twenty years after the witchcraft trials, the government insisted on rescinding the excommunications of the accused. 'To all intents and purposes, the power of theocracy in Massachusetts was broken.' (p. 127)

Although Miller does not record certain other details, it is of interest that Reverend John Hale, the man of learning who grew to have serious doubts about the presence of witches, published a book in 1697 in which he concluded that the whole proceedings had been based upon a fundamental error of judgement. In this he was anticipating the verdict of history. But from such a fundamental error a great deal of human suffering was caused, as Hale had tried to communicate to the Deputy Governor:

There are orphans wandering from house to house; abandoned cattle bellow on the highroads, the stink of rotting crops hangs everywhere, and no man knows when the harlots' cry will end his life. (p. 114)

Some few survived this destructive potency by chance. Of these, Elizabeth Proctor was one. She gave birth to the child which saved her life approximately two weeks after her husband's execution; she married again four years later and her descendants live to the present day in the United States.

FACSIMILE OF JOHN PROCTOR'S SIGNATURE

Extension projects:

(a) Consider how you would stage the play if you were asked to undertake a producer's responsibilities. It may be easier to think of specific encounters in the drama, such as the conversation between John and Elizabeth at the beginning of Act Two, the admission of John's adultery and Elizabeth's public lie in the courtroom (Act Three), John's final meeting with Elizabeth and his judges in Salem jail (Act Four).

(b) Construct, for discussion purposes, arguments on the advantages a non-naturalistic staging might have over a naturalistic staging.

Questions:

1. 'I believe that the common man is as apt a subject for tragedy in its highest sense as kings were.' (Arthur Miller)
   Discuss the implications of this statement
   (a) in general terms
   (b) in relation to the figure of John Proctor.

2. 'The power of the human will to overcome the forces of evil . . . lies at the centre of Miller's concept of tragedy.' (John Prudhoe, 'Arthur Miller and the Tradition of Tragedy', *English Studies*, Volume 43 (1962), pp. 430–439.)

   Consider the significance of this comment in a discussion of the themes Miller dramatizes in *The Crucible*.

3. John Proctor's 'progression is from a common sense wounded by his environment, through greater self-knowledge, towards a just, moral evaluation of himself.' (C. J. Partridge)

   Construct arguments, containing detailed references to the play, to demonstrate your measure of agreement or disagreement with this assertion.

4. Proctor's final dilemma is that 'there is no middle ground of private involvement and public neutrality.'

   Amplify the meaning of this statement by detailed references to the final acts of the play and show the extent to which you agree with it.

5. 'Although Proctor's body is destroyed, his conscience lives on. Thus, by their denials of guilt, he and the other martyred citizens force the law itself on trial.'

   Discuss in detail particular encounters by which Miller dramatizes this paradoxical reality.

6. 'John Proctor wavers between principle and com-

promise. Danforth is unyielding about the inviolability of principle.'

Make your own definitions of these statements in order to describe the tensions between the two men in the final acts of the play.

7. 'It is what transpired in the souls of John and Elizabeth Proctor that finally matters, and to that degree *The Crucible* is . . . a tragedy.' (John Gassner, *Theatre at the Crossroads*, Holt, Rinehart and Winston, 1960, pp. 274–278)

Discuss the implications of this critical assertion.

8. A weakness in the play is that 'Proctor and his wife are swamped by such a multiplicity of secondary characters that the personal drama of maintaining integrity in the face of compounded evil and folly is often dissipated.' (John Gassner, *Theatre at the Crossroads*, Holt, Rinehart and Winston, 1960, pp. 274–278)

To what extent do you agree with this criticism?

9. 'Rebecca Nurse resembles the very man who condemns her to be hanged. Like Danforth, she would not sacrifice a principle even if it should cost her her life.' (Edward Murray, *Arthur Miller, Dramatist*, Frederick Ungar Publishing Co., 1967, p. 69)

Discuss the similarities and differences of these characters.

10. 'The denouement in the trial scene has true tragic inevitability.'

Make your own definition of 'tragic inevitability' and, in the light of your definition, analyse Act Three to determine the validity of this assertion.

11. '*The Crucible* is a tragedy and its theme is that men, no matter how erring, are capable of enduring everything for their sense of decency.' Discuss.

12. 'The message of the play is that hysteria is always with us and that vigilance is constantly necessary.'

How adequate is this deduction about *The Crucible's* dramatic significance?

13. 'The major question Miller asks in the play is: How should a man act in the face of evil?'

How adequate is this deduction about *The Crucible's* dramatic significance?

14. '*The Crucible* was not meant to be merely a mirror held up to the Un-American Activities Committee; it was meant to explore pure evil, evil as wholehearted as Iago's.' (T. C. Worsley, 'American Tragedy', *The New Statesman and Nation*, 23 August, 1958, p. 220)

Compare Iago in Shakespeare's *Othello* with Deputy Governor Danforth in *The Crucible*.

15. 'The dialogue of the play is a considerable accomplishment. It suggests the flavour of seventeenth century speech without becoming distractingly archaic and without sacrificing simplicity, strength, or suppleness.' (Robert Hogan, *Arthur Miller*, University of Minnesota Pamphlets on American Writers, p. 30)

By discussing specific examples of dialogue show the extent of your agreement with this description.

16. '*The Crucible* is one of those rare plays in which the writing is fundamentally poetic.'

Define this comment and discuss its implications by analysis of specific examples.

17. By detailed analysis of *either* Act Three *or* Act Four write an essay on Miller's use of dramatic irony.

18. To what extent does Miller employ foreshadowing of events as a structural device in *The Crucible*?

19. Analyse the dramatic structure of *The Crucible*.

20. 'One watches *Death of a Salesman* to discover what a man is like, but one watches *The Crucible* to discover what a man does.'

By detailed references to the two plays, discuss the implications of this statement.

FURTHER READING

The following is a list of Arthur Miller's plays and the dates of their first production in the United States. It should be noted that his *Collected Plays* (published 1957) does not include the work of Miller's second period which begins with *After the Fall*.

All My Sons (1947)
Death of a Salesman (1949)
An Enemy of the People (adapted from the play by Henrik Ibsen, 1950)
The Crucible (1953)
A Memory of Two Mondays (1955)
A View from the Bridge (1955)
After the Fall (1964)
Incident at Vichy (1964)
The Price (1968)

Indirect references have been made in the text of this book to the undermentioned critical works. They are listed for convenience. Students of *The Crucible* should accept their analyses and conclusions only *after* personal scrutiny of the play itself and *after* individual thought about the quality of arguments offered by critics. A major work of art invariably creates a greater totality than any single critic can encompass in his ruminations, articles, or books.
Robert W. Corrigan (editor), *Arthur Miller: A Collection of Critical Essays*, Prentice-Hall, Inc. (New Jersey), 1969.

Robert Hogan, *Arthur Miller*, University of Minnesota Pamphlets on American Writers, 1964.

Sheila Huftel, *Arthur Miller: The Burning Glass*, The Citadel Press New York), 1965.

Leonard Moss, *Arthur Miller*, Twayne Publishers, Inc. (New York), 1967.

Edward Murray, *Arthur Miller, Dramatist*, Frederick Ungar Publishing Co. (New York), 1967.

Gerald Weales (editor), *Death of a Salesman: Text and Criticism*, The Viking Press (New York), 1967. (This contains Miller's important article 'Tragedy and the Common Man', pp. 143–147.)

Dennis Welland, *Arthur Miller*, Oliver and Boyd (Edinburgh), 1961.

NOTES ON ENGLISH LITERATURE

Chief Adviser: JOHN D. JUMP, *Professor of English Literature in the University of Manchester*

General Editor: W. H. MASON, *Sometime Senior English Master, The Manchester Grammar School*

1 **Macbeth** (Shakespeare)
JOHN HARVEY

2 **The Prologue** (Chaucer)
R. W. V. ELLIOTT, *Professor of English, Flinders University, South Australia*

3 **Murder in the Cathedral** (T. S. Eliot)
W. H. MASON

4 **Pride and Prejudice** (Austen)
J. DALGLISH, *Sometime Senior English Master, Tiffin School*

5 **Twelfth Night** (Shakespeare)
BARBARA HARDY, *Professor of English, Birkbeck College*

7 **Wuthering Heights** (Emily Brontë)
BARBARA HARDY

8 **The Mayor of Casterbridge** (Hardy)
G. G. URWIN, *Senior English Master, Sale Grammar School for Boys*

9 **Jane Eyre** (Charlotte Brontë)
BARBARA HARDY

10 **St. Joan** (Shaw)
W. H. MASON

11 **Nostromo** (Conrad)
C. B. COX, *Professor of English Literature, University of Manchester*

12 **Absalom and Achitophel** (Dryden)
W. GRAHAM, *Sometime Senior English Master, Dame Allan's Boys' School, Newcastle-upon-Tyne*

13 **The Rivals, The School for Scandal, The Critic** (Sheridan)
B. A. PHYTHIAN, *Langley Park School for Boys, Beckenham*

14 **King Lear** (Shakespeare)
HELEN MORRIS, *Principal Lecturer in English, Hamerton College, Cambridge*

15 **A Passage to India** (Forster)
W. H. MASON

16 **The Nun's Priest's Tale and the Pardoner's Tale** (Chaucer)
R. W. V. ELLIOTT

17 **Paradise Lost, Books IV and IX** (Milton)
W. GRAHAM

18 **King Richard II** (Shakespeare)
HELEN MORRIS

19 **Men and Women** (Browning)
MARK ROBERTS, *Professor of English Literature, University of Belfast*

20 **The White Devil, The Duchess of Malfi** (Webster)
JOHN D. JUMP, *Professor of English Literature, University of Manchester*

21 **Middlemarch** (George Eliot)
A. O. COCKSHUT, *Fellow of Hertford College, Oxford*

22 **The Winter's Tale** (Shakespeare)
G. P. FOX, *Lecturer in English, Department of Education, University of Exeter*

23 **Sons and Lovers** (Lawrence)
CHRISTOPHER HANSON, *Lecturer in English Literature, University of Manchester*

24 **Sylvia's Lovers** (Mrs. Gaskell)
GRAHAM HANDLEY, *Senior Lecturer in English, All Saints' College, Tottenham*

25 **Antony and Cleopatra** (Shakespeare)
HELEN MORRIS

26 **The Prelude I & II** (Wordsworth)
W. GRAHAM

27 **Howards End** (Forster)
G. P. WAKEFIELD, *Senior English Master, King George V School, Southport*

28 **Persuasion** (Austen)
J. R. COATES, *Senior English Master, Hymer's College, Kingston-upon-Hull*

29 **To the Lighthouse** (Woolf)
W. A. DAVENPORT, *Lecturer in English, Royal Holloway College*

30 **Man and Superman** (Shaw)
A. W. ENGLAND, *Senior Lecturer in English, Eaton Hall College of Education, Retford, Notts.*

31 **Riders to the Sea, Playboy of the Western World** (Synge)
A. PRICE

32 **Childe Harold III and IV, Vision of Judgement** (Byron)
PATRICIA BALL, *Lecturer in English, Royal Holloway College*